The Broken Pearl

That became part of the Crown.

By Reba Mason

The Broken Pearl is a collection of spiritual prayers. Names, characters, places, and incidents can be based on facts. Any resemblance to actual people, living or dead, events, or locales is purely coincidental.

Published by Books Sphere LLC

www.bookssphere.com

Grand Junction, CO.

ISBN: 978-1-968766-15-3

First Edition: 2026

Printed in the United States of America

The Broken Pearl

That became part of the Crown.

Bringing you into the teachings from God, Jesus, and the Holy Spirit that I experienced during the last few years, and the text messages I sent from Him to my children and grandchildren about Him and life through Him.

Reba Mason

Preface

"For we are His workmanship, created in Christ Jesus for good works, which God prepared beforehand, that we should walk in them."
Ephesians 2:10 ***ESV***

Many years ago, in fact, it was about 10 years ago, I had the opportunity to attend a bible meeting. It wasn't just any ordinary meeting; it was a Prophetic gathering. After a few minutes of worship, and a brief message, everyone attending was given a 3x5 index card, so if they wanted a prophecy spoken over them to write down some information about themselves. Such as name, age, and if memory serves me correctly what we did for a living. Eager to know if God had a special prophesy for me, I filled out the card and waited for my turn. I really don't remember anything about my prophecy except I would write a book. My thoughts, yeah, right! A dirt road raised farm girl. Finished high school, worked my way through adult education courses for my job requirement to advance my knowledge about my job, but never entertained that I would ever arrive at this level. Well fast forward 10 years to today. I now realized that God had brought me to writing this book. Writing this came out of a particular circumstance that a precious grandchild of mine was going through.

Very concerned over her situation God instructed me one morning to text a message He had given me. It was in generalities, no pointing fingers, no name calling. The next day God gave me another message. By the third day He said title each day with a heading topic, such as Mondays Meditation, Tuesdays Tips and so on for each day. For over a year, almost each day, I have given my children and grandchildren what I believe to be a message from God. These messages were not just for them, but for me also. God wanted me to not only get closer to Him, but to teach me His ways, who He is, how He loves me and wants to spend time with me. You see, growing up without a father in my life I had a terrible time getting the concept of what a true father was like. Now, you have my reason for writing this book. I have had the awesome privilege of spending time with my Father, and Lord. A Father I truly never knew because I never had an example of one in my life.

So, I want to thank those of you who are reading this book. I am so glad you want to delve into the life that God has taught me. In the following pages of this book, you will learn of the many thoughts and teachings I have been given from God over these past several months. I also believe He wanted me to share these messages with my children, as well as you and those of the next generations.

I pray these thoughts inspire, encourage and teach you the ways of God that He taught me. Hopefully, these following pages will change you and your view of who God is and how He views, works and thinks about His creation, you. My prayer is that this book will produce in you a stronger desire for a more intimate relationship with your Father God, Jesus the Christ, your King and Lord and God's Holy Spirit. If you don't know Him, but have come to believe He is the crucified, risen Son of God, just ask Him to become your Savior. It's that simple, and He will never turn down anyone who believes He is God's Son and wants Him to be their Lord and Savior. He created you just to spend time with you. How awesome is that? As I began this journey I, myself, learned so many truths of who the Father, Son and Holy Spirit are. And I never realized life could be so beautiful with Him. My earthly eyes could not see who He truly was. I had to develop a personal relationship with Jesus to acquire my spiritual eyes to see Him. And I do mean a personal, one on one, relationship.

Those of you who are about to read these pages, I ask that you first stop and ask to be a child of God through Christ Jesus and then let Him open your spiritual eyes to see Him as He did mine. If you realize nothing else as you read this book, I pray that you understand you are here ONLY because God wanted you and wanted to be your Father. Because of His great love for me, I love you. If you find out who God truly is through these next pages and how much He loves you, you will never be the same again, and my reason for writing this book will have accomplished its purpose. A soul saved. An intimate relationship with the Father. Blessings and favor, I give you.

Reba Mason

Dedication

I first want to dedicate this book to my WONDERFUL husband, Jimmy. I love you, thank you. You are and have been my love, my support and encouragement in all my endeavors in life. Next are my beautiful daughters, Wanda Cochran and LeAnn Reynolds, I love you. Each one of you has made my life more beautiful than I could have ever asked. Thank you for putting up with me. Also, to my AMAZING sons-in-laws, Bob Cochran and Travis Reynolds. I love you dearly. You are my sons through Christ Jesus through marriage to my daughters. As this book goes to press, I also dedicate this to my 12 grandchildren and 24 great-grandchildren and to Keely, my precious granddaughter, who is now the first in our family to meet Jesus, face to face. Thank you for the blessing you gave us during the 3 years of your life here on earth. I know you are applauding us from heaven to keep going, never to give up, and to keep our faith in Jesus.

Truly By His Grace I Live, Breath, and Move.

Accepted And Loved

Monday's Meditations: Our Benefits

Bless the Lord, O my soul, and forget none of His benefits. Psalms 103:2 NASB

When you go to work, you are given benefits. Salary...sick leave...vacation...insurance etc. But you have to ACCEPT the job, in order to receive those benefits.

What about God's benefits. When you ACCEPT Christ Jesus as your Lord, you receive benefits. His benefits come under the atonement. They are redemption...Salvation...Holy Spirit gifts...deliverance and healing to name a few.

NOTE: You are just as redeemed as you are delivered, just as much healed as you are saved.

Question: If you are fully saved, are you partly healed? I don't think so.

Blessings.

I love you.

Tuesday's Tips: Talking Thoughts.

It's the thoughts that come into our heads that talk to us. Where do they come from?

Genesis 3. Satan begins to talk to Eve. Picture this: Satan slithering around in the garden swinging his tail like a big dude telling Eve, "Are you kidding me?" Do you really believe that junk God told y'all about the fruit on this lovely tree? Now look at Job 1. Who was it that went to heaven and complained about Job? Watch who's talking to you. Wouldn't that tell us to look carefully at what is being said in your thoughts.

2CORITHIANS 10:5 NIV …We are to destroy every thought and lofty thing that is raised up against what we know God said, and take those thoughts captive, give them to Jesus, so we will be in obedience to what God says about us. Think on the things that He says about you and not what others say.

And don't believe that Job is the only one Satan complains to God about.

I bless you and honor you today...Memaw

Forever Loved by Jesus

Wednesday's Word: What Will You Do With The Word?

Psalms 118 24. NIV... Today is the day the Lord has made

It's your choice. My prayer is that every text I send, you will see with your heart that every word read is Jesus talking with you one on one. And not me.

Did you know that you are His life? That every beat of His heart is beating for you?

Yesterday, during worship at Highlands Church they sang a song I couldn't remember singing before. Maybe it's a new one. But three words in that song stood out like a mountain. The words were "honor His love." No matter what happens today, honor His love. No matter what is said to you, honor His love.

Jesus said to me last night and again this morning. No one being ugly to another person of My creation deserves love. And in our flesh, we can't love the unlovable. So, I want you to give them the love I gave you. Especially the love I gave you when you were ugly. Today is the day the Lord has made, will you choose to Honor His Love?

Loving you with the beat of His heart...Memaw

He Was Wounded

Thursday's Thoughts: Wounded And Bruised

...but He was wounded for our transgressions.... He was bruised for our iniquities...the chastisement of our peace was upon Him...and with HIS stripes we ARE healed. Isaiah 53:5. KJV

Glory

Transgressions: is when we have stepped out of bounds into another person's life and offended them by insulting, embarrassing, or humiliating them in some way.

Iniquities: that's the condition of our hearts. The things we say or do that portray who we really are.

Chastisement: the beating Jesus took on Himself for the sins we commit so we can walk around in peace knowing we won't have to take the beatings for our own sins.

One more thought. Sin is actually doing what God says not to.

Can you see what Jesus did just because He wants to be in your life?

Be the glory of Jesus today. I love you...Memaw

The Sabbath Is Holy

Friday's Fruit: Keeping The Sabbath

Blessed the sabbath and keep it holy

Yesterday, as Bob and I were talking, he said one of the most profound truths I have heard in a long time. He said: Miracles should be the normal thing happening around us. Instead of being shocked when we see a miracle happen, we should be shocked if they don't.

Now think about what he said. Miracles should be happening daily, and we should not be surprised.

Love you ALL Memaw

Blessed Of Our Father and Lord Jesus

Saturday's Sayings: Who Is In Control Of You?

Love...joy...peace...patience…kindness...goodness...faithfulness... gentleness, and self-control. Galatians 5:22-23 NLT.

The Living Bible says: Verse 22....when the Holy Spirit CONTROLS our lives, He will PRODUCE these kinds of fruit in us.

Verse 19...but when we follow our own wrong inclinations, our lives will PRODUCE these results: evil results, impure thoughts, eagerness for lustful pleasure, idolatry, complaints and criticisms, envy.... (And about 11 other sins that are mentioned through verse 21)

Question: What is the fruit in your thoughts and actions today, and where are they coming from, the Holy Spirit or ???

Verse 16...obey the Holy Spirit's instructions. He will tell you where to go and what to do. Thank you, Jesus, for the Holy Spirit.

From the Word of God.... and the love of Memaw

Reconciliation Of God

Sunday's Song: Anyone Want A Miracle?

2 Corinthians 5:18-19 NKJV. Now all these things are from God, who reconciled us to Himself through Christ and gave us the ministry of reconciliation, namely, that God was in Christ reconciling the world (me) to Himself, (listen) not counting their (my) trespasses against them (me) and He has committed to us (me) the word of reconciliation.

Whoa, what a miracle. But the miracle that begins reconciliation is forgiveness.

Let me describe how I believe God described it to me. There are 3 levels or degrees in forgiveness.

Let's start at level 3, which is asking someone to forgive you. It's awkward, uncomfortable, and somewhat embarrassing.

Admitting you were wrong can be humbling.

Level 2 is receiving forgiveness, and this is hard because you feel you don't deserve to be set free so easily. You feel you need punishment instead of freedom.

Now, to level 1 this one is the hardest because your hurt is so real and painful. And it is both. But the flesh has a very hard time giving those who hurt you, their freedom. The flesh feels they don't deserve it. And they probably don't, but neither did I, but I got it. I am clean as a newborn baby. And if you don't receive your forgiveness from Christ and give it to those who hurt you, you will never be at peace. I promise you on God's Word you will become a new person when you forgive.

Now, do you want to be free, then forgive, or you will be the one suffering, and not the offender.

I love you ALL SO VERY MUCH. Memaw in Christ

Rejoice...Yesterday Is No More

Monday's Meditations: Rejoicing In Who You Are

John 15:5-6 NIV...I am the vine; you are the branches. If you remain in me and I in you, you will bear much fruit; apart from me you can do nothing. If you do not remain in me, you are like a branch that is thrown away and withers; such branches are picked up, thrown into the fire and burned.

Believers can and should walk, talk and spend time with Jesus every day. In fact, you can spend as much time with Christ as the disciples. Think about the stories the Bible tells us about the disciples spending time with Jesus. Picture this: you and Jesus, walking along together talking, listening and enjoying your time together. All of a sudden you spot a crowd of friends laughing, telling jokes, hearing them mention certain people's names and in your interest in what they are saying you take off for the group. They are telling ugly jokes. Mocking people about how they are dressed or their looks or something they did. Cursing and ridiculing their peers, and neighbors. Then you look back and Jesus isn't with you. He can't go with you. It isn't His standard of living or lifestyle to do harm to the very ones He created. He is standing where you left Him.

Choose today who you want to walk with.

Love you

Blessed Are You Lord

Tuesday's Tips: Walking Daily With Christ

Yesterday, Wanda sent us a powerful word about the hurt and angry feelings people have. So, I believe I need to step up to the plate to ask you something very important.

So dear Bob, Wanda, Travis, Lee, JJ, Leah, Will, Shane, Dyana, Elizabeth, John, Daniel, Ericka, Erin, Trent, Will, Corey, Tessa, Nathan, Garrett. I ask you to forgive me for every hurtful comment, all painful jokes...any insulting remarks...and any way that I acted before you that was not godly. I am SO sorry. I repent of everything you know I did to you. I love each of you and have the highest respect and honor for you. You are more valuable to me than any gold wealth and clout. I promise to strive to show you just how important and beautiful you are to me.

I love you as Christ loves me.

Please accept my deepest apology.

Memaw

Praise To You Jesus

Wednesday's Word: The Spirit's Personality

Galatians 5:22 list the Fruit not fruits of the Spirit of God. Fruit here means that everything listed in this verse is the Spirits personality. His entire being is made up of these beautiful qualities.

Verse 25 says IF we live by the Spirit, we should walk by the Spirit. Walking by the Spirit means to live a lifestyle just like His. Peace is one of the Spirit's personalities. Peace, the inner calming that comes from being assured of your salvation and relationship with Christ.

Take a deep breath and go get your Fruit on.

Love and joy...Memaw

A Life Worth Living

Thursday's Thoughts: Living Through Jesus

Do any of you have $5.00 you are willing to give me? If you answer yes, and you give it to me, then it doesn't belong to you anymore. It's mine to do as I want to. That's how you give your life to Jesus. It's His life living through you. Will life then be peaches and cream? Was Jesus's life on earth that way? The Bible says He was ridiculed, slandered, lied about, and even crucified. But I would still give up my life for His because He won, and I know I have also.

"Give away your life; you'll find life given back but not merely given back - given back with bonus and blessing. Giving, not getting, is the way. Generosity begets generosity." Luke 6:38 Message Bible

Think about whose life you'd rather have.

Love you above all.

Everything Is Seed

Friday's Fruit: Seed And Sowing

God said everything alive, plant...animal or reptile came from a Seed. The Seed of creation. Some seeds we eat are the actual seed itself. Peas, beans, corn and some things we eat are the product of the seed, such as apples, pears and watermelon. God's people being from the seed of Abraham produces seed. My question: what does your seed produce? I am talking about the seed of the spirit or heart. Does your seed produce anger, jealousy, envy, impatience and pride? Or does it produce love, joy, peace, kindness and forgiveness? And last who planted your seed? The world or the Word?

Look at your seed and examine what it is Sowing.

Love you by His love.

Revealing Jesus

Saturday's Sayings: Looking Like Jesus

Galatians 5:22.... but the Fruit of the Spirit is LOVE (even if it takes all you have, it's your character revealed) JOY (regardless of your circumstances) PEACE, KINDNESS, PATIENCE, GOODNESS, FAITHFULNESS, GENTLENESS, and SELF-CONTROL.

May your joy in all situations be revealed looking like Jesus.

I love you all. Memaw the mediator

Ponder Your Thoughts

Sunday's Song: What Do You Know?

Do you know all about sports?

Do you know how to fix things?

Do you know about Jesus?

A young man once said...you can't tell anyone about something that you don't know. He was referring to the Holy Spirit. How many times have you told someone about Jesus because you know Him? Do you know His will? You can find God's will about Jesus in every page of His Word.

Now ponder your thoughts on this: And this is the confidence that we have in Him that if we ask anything according to His will, He hears us, and if we know that He hears us, we know that we have the request that we asked of Him.

1JOHN 5:14-15. ESV

If you know Jesus, if you know Him, He hears you. If you know His will. Then you know He answers your request.

Simple....just a thought. Love you beyond words.

Corruptible Or Incorruptible

Monday's Meditations: What's Your Conscious Like?

God's Word says in 1Peter 1:23 KJV. Being born again not of corruptible seed but of incorruptible by the WORD of God which liveth and abideth FOREVER.

God longs for a personal relationship with each of His children. But it's hard for us to have that because Satan keeps reminding us of our sins. We have a hard time going to God in belief because we still feel guilty of the things we did in the past. But Jesus' blood makes our conscience righteous before God, not guilty. We are not guilty of our sins anymore. We are brand new kids. In the name of Jesus, don't let Satan destroy your relationship with your Father by reminding you of your past. Come boldly to your Father and tell Satan not today. God's Word doesn't respond to unrighteousness only righteous children and Jesus made that happen for us.

Glory....blessings, peace, honor, and grace, lovely children.
Memaw

God's Grace

Tuesday's Tips: Parents

Let me tell you my view of a dad and a child. Don't worry, I will get to moms later. The view a child has about his daddy is strength, he can pick up the world, security, dad is always the place to run to. Safety where I don't feel alone. Wisdom dad knows as much as God. He can fix everything. Trustworthy dad is my dependable rock. Sometimes he keeps my secrets. Hey, this is my child's vision of a dad; you will have to get your own.

Now to moms. Moms know everything. They have a very deep ESPN. Mom knows when her child is happy by his giggle. Mom knows when her child is sick by his demeanor. Mom knows when her child is hurt by his cry. Mom knows when her child has pooped. There is no other smell like it. She can smell his poop in a crowd of 100 kids. Mom knows when her child is doing something wrong by his silence. His silence is very loud in a mom's ears. She can hear it from next door. Wrap all these characteristics together, and you have a complete parent.

Don't let man put it asunder or you won't have a complete child. You are the best sweetest, beautiful children God gave to a mom.

My last Meditation. When my children married, they became ONE with their spouse. And that spouse became ONE to me. If my child will always be my child no matter what, then their spouse will always be mine no matter what.

Blessings, grace, and honor, I speak over you today. Memaw

Christ Like

Wednesday's Word: Christian Means....Christ- Like

If you were arrested for being a Christian, what evidence would they have against you?

The reason we don't live for Jesus is because it might cost us something. For example: as a Christian at work your boss tells you not to talk about Jesus, read your Bible at work or your fired. Who pays the price, Jesus or your job? Would being Christ like at work cost you something?

Jesus says: Under the law of Moses the rule was, 'if you kill, you must die.' But I have added to that rule, and tell you that if you are only angry, even in your own home, you are in danger of judgment. (WOW) If you call your friend an idiot, you are in danger of being brought before the court. And if you curse him, you are in danger of the fires of hell. Matthew 5:21-22. TLB

Living for Christ is a daily sacrifice...it will cost you. Are you prepared for it?

Because of His sacrifice...I love you...Memaw

Morning, Precious Children.

Thursday's Thoughts: Just A Thought

Luke 1:20... And behold, thou shalt be dumb, and not able to speak, until the day that these things shall be performed, because thou believest not my words, which shall be fulfilled in their season. KJV

Let's look at the word "dumb" in this verse. Zechariah has just been told by the angel Gabriel who stands in the presence of God listening for a command from God to go tell someone something. We'll talk about angels another time. But Gabriel tells Zechariah that he and Elizabeth are going to have a baby in their old age. But Zechariah questions Gabriel. And his question is one of doubt. We know this because Gabriel said "Because you doubt what I tell you God says, you will be struck dumb." Most of us know this means he can't speak. And that is true. Zechariah was unable to speak a word until John was born and given his name. But think a little deeper. The word dumb can also mean bewildered overwhelmed or stunned in mind and heart. If we are not careful to believe all God's promises for us, we become dumb, and if we refuse to let God show us the truth, we become dumber. Get it dumb and dumber.

Just a thought. Love you all tremendously.

Blessings from Jesus…Memaw

The Seed Of The Fruit

Friday's Fruit: Your Fruit Reveals Something

We cannot become what we need to be by remaining what we are.

Fruit- anything growing or grown. All Fruit contains a seed.

Galatians 5:22 The Fruit of the Spirit. Notice Fruit is singular, not plural. Fruit in God's Word describes His character that the Holy Spirit imparts. Fruit reveals character.

The first Fruit listed is LOVE. Love is not a feeling it's a decision as to how you treat people. If there is no love (seed) inside me...I will not possess any of the other characteristics. Everything begins with love. Even God's creation began because of love.

What does your Fruit taste like today? I love you.

1 more point...when we doubt, we can become dumbfounded, which sometimes causes us not to be able to speak.

Saturday's Sayings: Remembering

Remembering....remember the times you had that were happy, exciting, fun? Remember the times you were scared...hurt...disappointed? Remember the times that you did things that were stupid, mean, embarrassing? Remembering sometimes is good for the soul. Remembering the scary things makes you tremble. Remembering the stupid decisions, you wish you COULD forget but won't ever go away. Stupid decisions never go away. They are for a lifetime. And they hurt so many innocent people for their lifetime also.

I tell you this because I am one who made stupid decisions that I can't forget. But the ones that I remember that caused so much hurt and pain for others are my lifetime of consequences. Be kind and thoughtful and always live by God's standards so you will always have good memories.

From my heart I love you ALL so much.

Blessings From Jesus

Sunday's Song: Giving God Glory

Morning children. I love you. I have another sermon. I know I am talking to the choir. But even the choir needs to rehearse.

Your neighbor is not your enemy. Your coworker is not your enemy. Your spouse in your house is not your enemy. Your parents are not your enemy. News flash: Satan is.

When you say, I praise You Oh Holy God. I thank You Father for birthing me in America with my parents instead of mine fields, or garbage dumps to eat from. I give you glory for Jesus and Your Holy Spirit. I worship You, Lord God.

Then you are worshipping God.

By saying, I can't stand him/her. They are stupid. I wouldn't be caught dead with him/her. I hate my job, parents, siblings, spouse, and neighbors.

You are worshipping Satan.

Have a blessed day.

A Cup Of Water

Monday's Meditations: Here Comes The Sermon

Blessings and favor to each of you.

Today I am going to preach. So, listen.

Matthew 10:42 TLB: If, as my representative, you give a cup of cold water to a child, you will surely be rewarded.

So here is my cup of water to you as Jesus's representative for today. Matthew 10:38 NIV - if you refuse to take up your cross and follow me you are not worthy of being mine.

Explanation: if you use your problems, family, job, health, etc. as an excuse for not following every Word of Jesus. You are not worthy of being His. I am just telling you what Jesus said.

Mark 7:20 TLB - it is the thought life that pollutes. From within, out of man's heart come evil thoughts of lust, theft, murder, adultery, wanting what belongs to others, wickedness, deceit, lewdness, envy, slander, pride, and ALL other folly. These are the things that pollute you and make you unfit for God.

And last, before dawn this morning, Jesus described to me how God said what judgment day would be like. He said, If I have known or unknown sin in my life, I am unrighteous before Jesus. If I confess my sins before Jesus, He forgives me by covering me with His blood. It's between Jesus and me Nice.

But if I don't confess my sins to Him while here on earth, then come judgment day, there is no blood, no advocate. And I am standing before every person in the universe, for them to get to hear what I would not confess before this day. So, it's either between you and your Lord now, or it’s before the entire world later.

By the way. Later always shows up.

I love you all with my life. Amen

Prayers

Tuesday's Tips: Answered Prayer

I said, "Lord, if I could see You answer my prayers, I would believe more."

God said, "If I saw that you believed Me more, I would answer more."

Lovely...blessings...Memaw

Morning, My Precious Children.

Wednesday's Word: Seeing Great Things

I love you with all my heart. I see great things in each of you because God told me.

Jesus said: you were worth dying for. I love you more than my own life in the flesh. I can't wait for you and me to spend time together today.

As I was reading God's Word this morning, God said: Job never knew it was Satan who was hurting him, causing him pain, breaking his heart, making him sick, and trying to take his life. Think about it.

What could Satan be doing to your life?

BLESSINGS and peace…Memaw

Good Morning Father, Jesus And Holy Spirit

Thursday's Thoughts: Self-control

Yes, self-control is a Fruit of the Holy Spirit. The center or seed of the fruit of self-control is "Choice."

The word "choice" means to select or the act of making a decision. Since God chose us first, He commands us to choose. It is a command, but it boils down to: He just wants us to be like Him.

John 15:16 - God chose us

Joshua 24:15 - He says choose this day whom you will serve.

John 3:16 - for God so much loved you that He chose to give His ONLY Son so that whoever chose His Son will not perish.

Genesis 1:27 - God chose to create us to be like Him.

Romans 8:7 - for the mind that is set on the flesh (myself) is hostile to God.

1Corithians 15:33 - do not be deceived "bad company ruins good morals"

Be careful in choosing your Fruit today.

From God's Word and Memaw

I choose to be just like Jesus, even if it hurts my flesh.

From The Psalms

Friday's Fruit: Being His Servant

Sons and daughters, come and let me teach you the importance of trusting and fearing the Lord. Do you want a long, good life? Then watch your tongue! Keep your lips from lying, turn from all known sin, and spend your time doing good. Try to live in peace with everyone; Work hard at it.

From Memaw, the servant of the Most High God.

Thank You, Jesus, For ALL My Blessings

Saturday's Sayings: Your Knower

Morning chilluns. (that's southern for children) I love you

Your Knower is the place in your heart where true facts are undeniable.

For example: You know in your Knower that men are men by their body parts and women are women for the same reasons. Your Knower says these types of truths are unchangeable. I believe that's the type of faith God is looking for in His people. Not I wish or I hope God answers, but undeniable "I know" faith by what He said He will do. Abraham had a Knower faith. If you know God spoke it, your Knower should have no doubt. Read God's Word with your Knower and watch what happens.

My Knower loves you all.

Side note: The other day I told you about Sowing seed, and we were from the seed of Abraham. It's not his biological seed that we inherited, it was his seed of faith. Abraham willed us his Knower.

Amen

It's A New Day

Rejoice...Yesterday Is No More.

Sunday's Song: God's Protection

John 15:5 NIV...I am the vine; you are the branches. If you remain in me and I in you, you will bear much fruit; apart from me you can do nothing. If you do not remain in me, you are like a branch that is thrown away and withers; such branches are picked up, thrown into the fire, and burned.

I may have shared this story with some of you before, but just listen away.

In a small group meeting one night, a pastor who attended Rhema Bible College in Tulsa Oklahoma, told us this story.

One Sunday during worship, this pastor got a tap on his shoulder. He looked up and saw his son's worship leader. She leaned down and whispered, "Come with me." He got up and followed her. Thinking, what has he done now? She opened the door to the room and standing on the table was his 5-year-old son praying in tongues and all the children around the table were crying.

This couple finished College and came back home to Crenshaw County. Fast forward about 10-12 years. His boys are on their way to school after picking up a friend. It's and EXTREMELY foggy morning. But being in a hurry they followed a truck that was passing another vehicle. The truck ahead moved back into the right lane and immediately the boys hit head-on into an oncoming vehicle. Their truck broke in half upon impact. One son went through the windshield. The other son went under the truck through the floorboard, where the truck broke in half. At the hospital, both boys were very critical and not expected to survive. Being a man of faith who knew God deeply, and in his time alone with the Father, he asked him "why?" God said: they got out from under His protection. Meaning they didn't obey Him by keeping the laws of the nation. They were going too fast and passing in unsafe conditions. They survived the wreck, but both have scars today. One son even went to college after the 10th grade. Very intelligent, but the wreck left both their bodies somewhat crippled.

Message: Don't think that in everything you decide to do, God is protecting you. It may be something that He can't go with you in.

Think, ask, listen for God's reply before you move.

Loving you....Memaw

What A Glorious Day

Monday's Meditations: Use SOAP

S..stands for scripture. Like soap for your body...scripture cleanses, heals and refreshes a tired body, and soul. It makes you smell good. Ephesians 5:26, Psalms 30:2, Jeremiah 31:25, Ephesians 5:1-2.

O..observation...means to take heed to...to keep...to watch Isaiah 42:20

A..apply...use what God's Word says as your life. If you don't put your child's bicycle together, he can't ride it. If you don't apply God's Word, your life will be in pieces like the bike. Nothing works right. Luke 11:28

P..prayer..talking to God...not at Him. 1Thessaloians 5:16-17.

Have you used your soap today?

I love you...Memaw

It Is Written

Tuesday's Tips: Knock, Knock....Who's There?

If Jesus came to your house, knocked on the door, and handed you a gift box, and in the box was your healing. Would you receive it or hand it back and say no thank you I have a pill? Don't get me wrong, doctors and some medication is good. They are good for relieving the symptoms, but they do not heal you. Take your medication so you can focus better on thanking Jesus for healing you.

So today I want to tell you how I prescribe God's healing process.

First say, "Thank you, Jesus, that by Your stripes I am healed."

Then say, "It is written Satan, that by Jesus's stripes I am healed.

And last say, "And I believe that by Jesus's stripes I am healed."

By saying thank you, it is written and I believe according to His Word, morning, noon and night, so shall thou be made whole.

This prescription lasts until eternity.

Blessing's love and power in Jesus' name...Memaw

So Much Noise

Wednesday's Word: Psalms 91:3 KJV

Morning...have I told you today that I love you? Have I told you I need each of you? To all those born into my life and the ones who became mine because you said, "I DO," I love you.

Surely, He shall deliver you from the snare of the fowler and from the noisome pestilence.

Fowler means the devil, or it could be someone who entices you to sin.

Noisome pestilence means fatal, or grave disease or plague...it can also mean dangerous doctrine.

Plague is anything that causes trouble.

Now, let's put this into today's life. The hunter knows the habits of his prey. He learns their behavior and what it takes to lure them into the trap he has set for them. As a woman know how to shop. She knows how to find the best bargains. She learns the habits of the stores. She knows how to leap over 4 isles with a buggy and kids in toe to get that special item. The devil knows your habits, your behavior and he knows how to trap you. He knows by the way you have responded when you were unhappy, disappointed, angry, or not nice to others. He knows how to trap us by our fleshy appetites.

2CORITHIANS 2:11 ESV...so that we would not be outwitted by Satan, for we are not ignorant of his schemes. Be on guard...your enemy is lurking about seeking whom he may devour. If you know God, then you can recognize when Satan is around.

Love and grace...Memaw

Blessings And Peace With Joy In Christ.

Thursday's Thoughts: Forgiveness

Today is the day to forgive, or one day you will stand in the presence of Jesus, and He will ask, "Why?" - now what's your reason?

Put on the full armor of God.

Shield of faith: A barrier of trust and confidence in God that protects in danger or harm, knowing He will do what He says.

Gird your loins: Encircle your body with God's Word when things are difficult or challenging.

Shod your feet: Always being ready to go tell others about God.

Helmet of salvation: Your thinking is guarded or protected, knowing you are saved in Christ.

Ephesians 6:13-17

Forever His...I love you.. Memaw

Morning Blessed Children

Friday's Fruit: What Direction Are You Headed In?

If things seem to be upside-down in your life, you might be going in the wrong direction. God is never wrong. God has already done everything He is going to do. We just have to receive it. My faith grows as I use it.

Expect to hear...Expect to understand...Expect to see...that's faith. Believe everything God tells you.
Living by faith requires fighting. Not quitting. Keep believing what God says about you...not how much you failed.

1JOHN 5:4......whosoever is born of God...overcomes the world.

A person who is walking in Christ doesn't care what the world says or thinks about them.

Walk in the flesh, and you will fight in the flesh.

I love you and have faith in Jesus that you are the Victor.

Just saying Memaw

The Favor Of Jesus

Saturday's Sayings: You Are His Child

Trust in the LORD with all your heart and lean not on your own understanding; In all your ways acknowledge Him, and He shall direct your paths. Proverbs 3:5-6 NKJV

I don't know why this is so hard. But it is. I guess it is because we were raised on McDonald's standards. Order up, and we have it. Trust means to confidently rely on who you want something from. You are confident you're gonna get that sausage biscuit. But what about God? Where is your confidence in Him? He created you and gives you the air you breathe in order to stay alive. So, can't you trust Him with everything else? I learned the hard way. Trust is a choice. You have to exercise it in your life. Trust has to be lived every moment. Lean on Him. In fact, close your eyes and crawl up in God's lap and lean on Him. You are His child. It would delight Him to have you in His presence. He ALWAYS has your answer.

I love you...But God loves you even more.

I bless you with favor from Jesus today.

Memaw

In The Name Of Jesus

Sunday's Song: Praying His Word

Father in Jesus' name, I ask You as ...Psalms 86:11-13 TLB says. Tell me where you want me to go, and I will go there. May every fiber of my being unite in reverence to Your name. With ALL my heart I will praise You. I will give glory to Your name forever, for You love me so much! You are constantly so kind! You have rescued me from deepest hell.

Thank you, Father. Amen

Did you know you could pray God's Word for your needs, desires, and requests? And if you believe those Words of His, He WILL always answer you? Just believe what God says, and it's done.

Praying His Word over you today. I love you.... Memaw

P.S. God will NOT say no to His own Word.

Following Jesus

Monday's Mediations: Are you Following Jesus For The Wrong Reasons?

Mark 7...Mark 5...Matthew 9 and Luke 5

In these scriptures, Jesus heals a deaf man, a child, two blind men and a leper. But strictly told them not to tell anyone. Why? Because He didn't want people following Him for the wrong reasons.

There are people today who follow Jesus for the wrong reasons. But has anyone told them the right way?

What would you say if Jesus asked you why you were following Him? Following Jesus means you will be telling others about Him. When you do, be prepared to look weird to those around you. But who's life, do you wanna look good too? The world or Jesus?

Blessings Memaw

Hello My Children

Tuesday's Tips: I Love You

I love you so very much. I think of you daily and pray honor, grace, peace, love, blessings, prosperity, and more of God in your life. That each of you falls so fully in love with Christ that everyone you meet finds Jesus through you without you even opening your mouth. That they will know Him through you.

For God so loved that we should to. Memaw

Examine Yourself

Wednesday's Word: Faithfulness

Faithfulness means loyal, supportive, devoted to a person, cause, belief, or commitment. It's the actions of the heart and mind, to be dedicated to something or someone.

Faithfulness comes from a place of trust.

Its characteristics are love, patience, endurance, and long-suffering.

Learn to love, to be respectful, patient, and understanding. Don't get upset over small things. Learn to accept life itself as a gift from God, no matter how good or bad you think it is. Ask Jesus to do the work in your heart that needs to be done in order for you to reflect His character.

2 Corinthians 13:5 NIV

Examine yourselves to see whether you are in the faith; test yourselves. Do you not realize that Christ Jesus is in you—unless, of course, you fail the test?

Rejoice always...Memaw

The Righteousness Of God

Thursday's Thoughts: What Does My Faith Look Like?

Hallelujah to God…. Jesus and His awesome Holy Spirit.

Oh, what a glorious morning God has given us. I was awake most all-night listening to God. Oh, children, the things that He told me were awesome.

He talked with me about Facts and Faith. He said so much that it will take weeks to share. But I will try my best to keep it short for today.

1. Our faith has been hijacked by Satan, telling us that what we want to happen might not be God's will. Malarkey.

2. Looking at the facts, never changed anything. God said by faith in Me it shall be done.

3. Romans 12:3c... God has given us a measure of faith, and we get to use from Him, the measure He gave us.

Use 1/2 cup of faith… get a 1/2 cup of answer. Use overflow of faith… receive overflow of answer.

4. Faith is our will involved.

5. Our minds rely on facts. Our hearts rely on faith.

I will hush for now, but there is much, much more until later.

I love you forever just like Jesus....Memaw

Friday's Fruit: Facts or Faith

Psalms 55:22 NIV...cast your burden upon the Lord (by faith) and He shall sustain you. He will never let you fail.

Facts vs Faith

FACT: My cousin's wife has been diagnosed with breast cancer.

FAITH: In Jesus' name she is healed.

FACT: Sara was barren.

FAITH: Changed it… Isaac was born.

FACT: With God it can always be changed by faith.

FAITH: In God becomes truth in your soul.

FACT: Mountains are huge and enormous.

FAITH: In Christ can move our moutains into the sea.

Taste and see that God's Word is true.

I love you and honor you...Memaw

Receive It

Saturday's Sayings: According To Your Faith

Matthew 9:29 NIV...Jesus touched their eyes and said, "According to your faith, be it unto you."

Fact: You are a child of your parents.

Faith: In Christ you are a child of God.

Fact: Kenneth Hagan, a well-known minister of the Lord, was born crippled and had heart disease. At age 16, bedridden very close to death. In fact, they were planning his funeral.

Faith: using God's Word and believing it was true for him. Faith got him up on his feet and lived preaching until 83.

EVERY Word God has spoken is to you and directly for you.

Receive it. Blessings and so much love. Memaw

Children Are A Gift

Sunday's Song: News Flash

God said children are a gift, and each of you nailed it. I am the MOST blessed momma in the world. Glory to You, Jesus, for the children You have given me.

Facts vs Faith (again)

Fact: sin, diseases, sicknesses, trials, and problems are caused by Satan or through a decision we made.

Faith: I believe that ALL sin, diseases, sicknesses, trials, problems are healed through faith in Christ Jesus.

Face the facts or release faith.

Faith changes EVERY circumstance you don't want in your life.

You know things are changing in your relationship with God when in your subconscious, you find yourself singing to Him while you are doing something else or even thinking about your problems.

So beautiful.

I love you all SO VERY MUCH. News flash: God loves you more than I do.... from Glory to glory for Him...Memaw

Monday's Meditations: The Presence of Jesus

I praise Your Name, Jesus. I thank You, Father. Welcome, Holy Spirit.

Do you want to be in the presence of Jesus? Do you long to walk out your life with Him? If you do, you will have to change? When you are in His presence, you cannot live your life the way you do now. In God's Word, from Matthew...Mark...Luke and John, whoever came into the presence of Jesus, was changed. It wasn't always because He healed their diseases and sicknesses. It was because they said their life did not line up with His. Their beliefs didn't match His. Their desires didn't come close to His. Their decisions didn't correspond to His. And when they wanted Jesus in their life, they saw they were the ones who had to change. Would Jesus be with you in what you are going to do today? Would Jesus be sitting beside you, watching what TV programs you watch? Would Jesus be close by your side, listening to what you are saying to others, or about others, or even saying about yourself?

Psalms 25: ESV verses 4 – 8 – 9 -10

Verse 4 - show me the path where I should go.

Verse 8 - the Lord is good and glad to teach the proper path.

Verse 9 - He will teach the ways that are right and best to those who humbly turn to Him.

Verse 10 - and when we obey Him EVERY path, He guides us on is fragrant with His loving kindness and His truth.

This is the life you get when you want His presence with you.

I love you.

Oh, one more.

Verse 14...friendship with God is reserved for those who reverence Him.

Walking in Him...Memaw

I AM

Tuesday's Tips: Asking God

I ask God this morning what did He want me to tell mine and His kid's this morning. He said...tell them I AM love them so much.

Awesome. Love you forever. Memaw

Blessings...Peace...Joy

Wednesday's Word: The Lord Is Watching

Psalms 1:6 NLT... For the Lord watches over all the plans and paths of godly....

Psalms 9:10 TLB...All those who know Your mercy, Lord, will COUNT on You for help. For You have never yet forsaken those who trust in You.

God is expecting you to count on Him.

Psalms 18:30 TLB...What a God He is! How perfect in every way! ALL HIS promises prove true. He is a shield for everyone who hides behind Him.

I love HIS Word, and walk in His statutes. Memaw

Morning God's Children

Thursday's Thoughts: Thanking Jesus

Thank You, Father, for these amazing children You have given me. In Jesus' name. AMEN

This is what Christ Jesus did for me and you and everyone who receives Jesus as Lord of their lives. It's called The Atonement.

In other words, Jesus made everything in us right before God.

1. Redeemed...Jesus's life paid for the negative effects of your life called sin.

2. Salvation...power from Jesus's resurrection to live forever with Him.

3. Resurrection...raised to live with perfect bodies...cleansed and forgiven of ALL sin.

4. Freedom...from pain...sickness...temptation.

5. Forgiveness...EVERY sin is gone.

6. Eternal life...live in heaven with God

7. Repentance...asking for forgiveness and changing directions in my life.

8. Baptism in the Holy Spirit...your new friend and helper on earth and gifts from God.

9. Restoration ...EVERYTHING that Satan has taken away is given back.

10. Sainthood...holy...set apart for God.

11. Priesthood...priesthood is the power and authority that God gives to man to act in all things necessary for the salvation of God's children. The blessings of the priesthood are available to all who receive the gospel.

12. Grace...favor to receive the gifts and life God has for you.

13. Peace...calmness in things that normally would be upsetting.

14. Abundant Prosperity.

Isn't it awesome to live in Christ? Love you kids...Memaw

Thank you, Jesus for Your awesome love. Thank you, Holy Spirit for God's guidance and protection. Thank You Father for my life. Amen

I Love You Jesus

Friday's Fruit: Praising Jesus

I will praise the Lord no matter what happens. I will constantly speak of His glories and grace.

Psalms 34:1 TLB

I will instruct you, says the Lord, and guide you along the best pathway for your life. Psalms 32:8

How precious is Your constant love, O Lord. Psalms 36:7a

Bless the reading of Your Word O Lord God. That each one in this family believes with all their heart every word You speak. Amen and amen.

For His praise. Memaw

The Purpose Of God

Saturday's Sayings: For This Purpose

You are God's purpose. He created you for Himself, not the world. He only brought you into this world to receive His Son, Jesus, so He could have a personal relationship with you through Jesus and spend the rest of eternity with you. God has so many gifts for us. Your job is to accept them. When we go in another direction than the one God has purposed for us, we forfeit our gifts.

Satan also has a plan and purpose, and that's to kill, steal, and destroy you and your decision to follow the plan God purposed for you.

Jesus gave us His authority when He ascended back to His Father in heaven. If we don't use His authority and rebuke Satan's work, he will carry out his plans in your life. Jesus has already done everything we need for life here on earth. It's our responsibility to follow what He did.

For this purpose, the Son of God was manifested (revealed) that He might destroy the works of the devil. 1JOHN 3:8

Choose which side you want to be on.

I love you .... Memaw

Return, Repent

Sunday's Song: Before It's To Late

Psalms 32:3 TLB...there was a time when I would not admit what a sinner I was. But my dishonesty made me miserable and filled my days with frustration. TLB

Return to your God, your creator, before it's too late. There was a young couple with 2 children. Mid 20s. They accepted Christ and felt the call to go to ministry school. They sold everything. They only had their clothes, kids and a truck. He started school first. She saw his change and jumped in with Jesus. They returned home 2 years later. Eager to teach what they had learned, they took a divided church that the school taught them not to take. His wife wanted their ministry to be far away from their hometown. But he wanted to be back home. Disappointed, angry, and chewed on by church folks, she put it all down. Church, friends, family, husband, and began drinking. Fast forward 30 or more years. Today, they are sending her home from the hospital under hospice care. Sorosis of the liver and kidney failure.

The moral is, return to your God. Forgive others, forgive yourself. He asked us to pray for wisdom. I will. But I will pray what Jesus said also. If I could repent for her I would. I am brokenhearted that she decided no one or herself was worth forgiveness. All she wanted was to hurt others because they hurt her. A beautiful lady, a beautiful life taken by hurt anger and unforgiveness. I would love to ask her, was it worth it? I tell you this out of love for you. The fight to overcome hurt is a battle almost daily. But the outcome of the battle outweighs the years of agony and misery. I speak as a witness. I have been there, done that, and NEVER want that in my life again. I love you. I don't like preaching depressed stuff, but depressed stuff happens, and I refuse to keep quiet and let those I cherish to not hear the difference. I beg you, put whatever it is that's causing you hurt and pain down. All hurt, disappointment, and anger needs to be given back to Satan where it came.

Blessings, honor and grace...Memaw

Created Just For Us

Monday's Meditations: Loved, Blessed and Highly Favored

As I am walking around our neighborhood with Emma this morning. I looked around me and realized this vast earth God has created is for us. If you gaze into the sky, trees, hills and mountains, oceans and seas at what God has created it's just a small portion of the love God has for His people which is me and you. It's too big of a concept for me to grasp. He, God, Jesus, and the Holy Spirit loves me greater than the entire universe and all three heavens. Awesome. Amazing. As I stand here looking around seeing all that God did for me, I can't see one problem I have. It's like looking into the face of my Father, knowing He has got me, including my needs, my desires, and some of my wants. His Word somewhere says...ask me anything and I will do it. When you find it and as you read it, believe that it is true, but don't look for a time when God says He will do what you ask. The timing is not in there. It's because God wants you to trust Him until He does it. Then you will learn to love and trust Him more. Love and trust grow as you use them.

I bless you with favor, success, and honor before all men.

Love you Memaw

Tuesday's Tips: God's Power At Work

As I was searching in God's Word for help on peace and comfort, I found Ephesians 3:20-21 ESV that said: "Now to him who is able to do far more abundantly than all that we ask or think, according to the power at work within us, to him be glory in the church and in Christ Jesus throughout all generations, forever and ever. Amen"

What I had not noticed before was "God's Power At Work Within Us." Curious to know what that meant, I began searching and found a story from a book written by C.W. Loritts Jr. called "God's Got You Covered." It says:

"I recently took my ten-year-old nephew J.J. on a speaking engagement. He was overwhelmed when we got there. It was a huge auditorium, thousands of people were there, and television cameras were everywhere. It made me smile to see J.J.'s reaction to everything, but after a while, he asked me a question that made me chuckle. He looked at me with a look of concern on his face, and said, "Uncle C.W., do I need some money for food?"

"No, buddy," I said with a smile. "You don't need anything. The folks here have taken care of everything. As long as you're with me, you don't have need of anything."

It's a truth we take from the written Word of God that says: He has us covered! The apostle Paul addressed this issue when he wrote: "Now to him who can do far more abundantly than all that we ask or think, according to the power at work within us, to him be glory in the church and in Christ Jesus throughout all generations, forever and ever. Amen" (Ephesians 3:20)

What an amazing promise! This means that the same power that raised Jesus from the dead rests within us, ready to enable us to rise to any challenge we may face.

No matter what task is ahead, no matter what problem lies before you, God has promised that the power that lives within us through the Spirit of God is more than enough for us to emerge victorious."

Amen

"God's Got You Covered"
"Lessons From A Life Coach" by C.W. Loritts, Jr.

His Workmanship

Wednesday's Word: According To The Power At Work Within Us."

Since I am a day behind, I want to finish the article I just sent on Ephesians 3:20-21, which I was unable to include in my last post because of space:

"In these verses from Ephesians 3:20-21, the verb 'work" is in the present tense, meaning that God did not just do the work in us at the time we first received salvation, but continues to work within us. That's right! God's power is at work in you at this very moment.

I want to highlight three ways that God's power works within us:

The first is His conforming us to the image of His Son, meaning He is working in us to make us more like Jesus. God uses the problems we face in this life, combined with the power of His Spirit, to change us and make us into reflections of Christ.

The second way that His power works within us is by enabling us to do that which, in our own efforts, is impossible.

For example, that power enables us to overcome even the most stubborn habitual sin, and it enables us to speak with authority to others about the Lord Jesus Christ.

Third, that power is at work to sustain us. We all go through times of trouble and trial, times when we don't know what we are going to do next. The power of God works within us during those times to keep us and give us balance.

My friend Joseph Garlington likes to say, "God's power is getting you ready for what He already has ready for you." Another way to say that is, no matter what your needs are, no matter how desperate a situation, God is taking you through, you will always have the power to be victorious.

Always remember, God's got you covered!"

"God's Got You Covered"
"Lessons From A Life Coach" by C.W. Loritts, Jr.

I love you...Memaw

Thursday's Thoughts: His Presence Is Always With Me

You are the love of Jesus's life. He wrapped His entire life around you. He came to earth for no other purpose but you. Before you go out for your day's activities events, or work ask God in the name of Jesus for this:

Exodus 33:11-17 NIV...The LORD would speak to Moses face to face, as a man speaks with his friend. Then Moses would return to the camp, but his young aide Joshua, son of Nun did not leave the tent.

12 Moses said to the LORD, "You have been telling me, `Lead these people,' but you have not let me know whom you will send with me. You have said, `I know you by name, and you have found favor with me.'

13 If you are pleased with me, teach me your ways so I may know you and continue to find favor with you. Remember that this nation is your people."

14 The LORD replied, "My Presence will go with you, and I will give you rest."

15 Then Moses said to him, "If your Presence does not go with us, do not send us up from here.

16 How will anyone know that you are pleased with me and with your people unless you go with us? What else will distinguish me and your people from all the other people on the face of the earth?"

17 And the LORD said to Moses, "I will do the very thing you have asked, because I am pleased with you and I know you by name."

Become His friend, realize you have favor with Jesus, ask Him for His presence to go with you, so you will be distinguished from others as belonging to Him, and remember He knows you by your name. Beautiful.

Love you Memaw

Taking Your Thoughts Captive

Friday's Fruit: Perception

What is your perception of yourself, of others, or of God and Jesus?

Perception is a belief or opinion formed BEFORE enough information is available to make a correct or truthful answer.

Perception is when you make up in your mind in advance about something or someone without knowing the facts or truth.

2CORITHIANS 10:5 NIV...we demolish arguments and every pretension that sets itself up against the knowledge of God, and we take every thought captive to make it obedient to Christ.

What are your thoughts on? Are your thoughts on things that concern God...or yourself?

Matthew 16:22-23 – Peter was thinking of things of the world and not of Christ.

What if you took every thought captive? What if you refused to let any trash enter your mind? What if instead you took the counsel of God's Word, such as: above all else guard your heart, for everything you do flows from it. Proverbs 4:23 NIV

Your thoughts matter to God. Colossians 3:2 NIV says...set your mind on things above, not on things on the earth.

If you were to take every thought captive to Christ, how would it change your life?

Satan will have more control over you through your thought life. It's your choice...he can either gain control or lose control, it’s your decision. The very thing Satan wants is your peace. When you don't have peace, Satan has gained control.

Love you forever...Memaw

Saturday's Sayings: Good, Better, Best

There is a good...There is a better...but God has a best...a higher standard for us than we have yet attained. It is a better thing if it is God's plan and not ours.

When we please God in our daily service, we will always find that everyone who is faithful in the little things God will make ruler over much. Matthew 25:21

I love you all...Memaw

The Glory Of God

Sundays' Song: Do ALL

Whatever you do...do all to the glory of God...1Corithians 10:31 NIV.

It seems strange in our minds to think that we are the glory of a Holy God. But it's true if you have asked Jesus to be your Lord. You may not always do things that glorify Him but that doesn't change the fact of God's Word that with Christ as your Lord you are a glory to God. When I tell you what God's Word says about you, I can sense you can't believe it because you know what you have said in the past...you know what you have done...you know those places and people you should have never been involved with. But as a child of God through receiving God's Son as your Lord, you are now a glory to God. When your past shows up in your mind, it's Satan wanting to stop you from doing things that would look foolish to men, but glorify God. Take your stand, put on your salvation-forgiven cap, and do ALL to the glory of your Father God. You glorify God and He will honor you. Talk about Him like you talk about your favorite team, your family or yourself. Tell others good things about your Lord. Do you realize that the breath you just took in order to live belongs to Him? That's right, it was His air you breathed that was given to you. Take a deep breath and glorify your King.

Blessings with glory to Jesus...Memaw

Created Of God

Monday's Meditations: Disconnected

Ezekiel 37 describes how a person, church, business or family can be disconnected. Ezekiel was looking in a valley filled with bones. Dry divided bones. No life or connection was in any of this graveyard of bones. Then the Spirit of God came down. He brought muscles...tendons...breath...and life back into them. The Spirit reconnected every bone and inserted life into the circumstance. All those dry bones stood and were filled with purpose again.

Do you feel disconnected from something or someone? Ask the Holy Spirit of God to fill you with Himself today. But you have to purposely remove those things that have filled your heart and mind that are contrary to God's Word. Empty out the garbage and be filled full of the Lord. That's the only time you will have true life.

Read Ezekiel 37 and believe that God can bring life to your house again.

I love you...Memaw

His Hearts Desire

Tuesday's Tips: The Testimony Of Christ

Continuing with my last text from Ezekiel 37

And as I thought about my life and how God had done that very thing in me. He has taken a disconnected, lifeless, confused, guilt ridden, sinful person (me) and through His Word and awesome believers, He has brought me back to life in Him. I started this text messaging with you months ago. I know that the Holy Spirit was the one who brought this into being. But it is not for you as much as it is for me. You see, we are to be the testimony of Christ if we truly believe in Him. But until you become His best friend, there can't be much of a testimony about Him. There is not much you can tell people about Him if you haven't experienced a friendship with Him. How can you tell others what your child has done unless you have some experience to tell them? I had no testimony about Jesus until I wanted one. God can make a life where there is none. And that's my testimony. God is longing to bless you. His heart's desire is you. He never stops thinking about you. He waits for you to wake up and say, "Good morning, Jesus, I love you. What are doing today? Can I come with You?"

So that's my Tuesday's Tips for today...I get the awesome privilege of telling you what He did for me.

Blessing's Children

Wednesday's Word: His Ways Are Higher

For as the heavens are higher than the earth so are My ways higher than your ways and My thoughts than your thoughts. Isaiah 55:9 KJV

When we please God in our daily service, we will always find that everyone who is faithful in the little things God will make ruler over much.

You are in the right position when you allow the glory of the new life in Christ to cause you to act. Live in the Acts of the Apostles and every day you will see some miracle worked by the power of the living God.

Live, work and love for His Glory

I love you.... Memaw

His Law Doth He Meditate

Thursday's Thoughts: His Precepts

Nothing but the Word will do for every occasion. But this is what I need to do to receive His Word into my heart.

Psalms 119:33-40 KJV....teach me O Lord the way of Your statutes, and I shall observe it to the end.

Give me understanding that I may observe Your law. And I will keep it with all my heart.

Make me walk in the path of Your commandments. For I delight in it.

Incline my heart to Your testimonies and not to dishonest gain.

Turn away my eyes from looking at vanity and revive me in Your ways.

Establish Your Word to Your servant as that which produces reverence for You.

Turn away my reproach, which I dread, for Your ordinances are good.

Behold I long for Your precepts...revive me through Your righteousness. Amen

The Treasured Of God.

Friday’s Fruit: Thankful Sacrifice

Let's begin by thinking about your life. What's it like? Some will say it's the best I have ever had. Some might say it's the hardest life ever. But for those having a hard time remember that beautiful roses and flowers come out of hard ground. The great life comes from weathering hard trials. Sacrifices that come from giving your best for others...giving up your wants and desires for those that don't have is a true Sacrifice. Remember the story about the Gift and the Magi? He had a beautiful expensive watch that he adored. She had beautiful, long hair, which she loved. He gave his treasured watch to buy her a comb for her hair. She gave her long hair, for a chain for his watch. That's called a sacrificial gift. You give what you value and treasure most to someone who means the world to you. When you keep for yourself what you treasure most, it's your idol. What treasure do you have that you won’t give up for anything? When you give up your most valuable for others it becomes a treasure to them. If you keep your idol, that’s all the treasure you have. But be very careful with your idol because it will either be stolen or rot on you. And that is all you will end up with. I wonder what the impact of the story about the magi would have been if she gave her hair for his chain and he kept his beautiful watch because it was more valuable to him than his Sacrifice for her. Pretty sad. What stories are you leaving for others to tell, about you and your life? Jesus gave what we are supposed to give...our best...our life for others. Children, please find someone to whom you can give your best to. That's truly all they want...you. You see, you are God's treasure because He gave His treasure for you.

So thankful...Memaw

Angels Of God

Saturday's Sayings: Lessons About Angels

Today, I want to begin with some lessons about Angels. This will take several days, but I believe it's worth every second. Any second you get from God and His Word is always life-giving.

1. Angels were created by God just like you were created by Him. The only difference is they are only spirits, where we are spirits covered with fresh.

Colossians 1:16 ESV

2. Only three Angels names are recorded in our Bible. Michael, Gabriel and Lucifer. Michael is the chief angel. He is a warrior and messenger. Gabriel always gives a prophetic message. Michael came to do battle with evil forces trying to prevent Gabriel from giving Daniel a message from God.

In Ezekiel 16:11 NIV, says Lucifer who is Satan. Yes, Satan was once in heaven as God's worship leader. He was the most beautifully adorned angel God created. But he wanted God's position and was cast from heaven along with many other Angels who agreed with him. Now he is on earth, trying to get you not to live for God.

3. Angels are ministering spirits sent to serve those who will inherit salvation. Hebrews 1:7 KJV

Angels are watching over us. In Christ we have the privilege of calling on the Angels of the Most High God to come help, protect and guide us throughout our life. Angels are waiting to minister to you. Ask, in Jesus' name for their help. You will be amazed. But caution...Angels are NOT to be worshiped. Only Jesus and God are to be worshiped. Amen.

Stay tuned for more in Christ...love you Memaw.

God's Plan

Sunday's Song: Praising God With The Angels

Exodus 23:20 NIV- See I am sending an angel ahead of you to guard you along the way and to bring you to the place I have prepared.

For He will order His angels to protect you wherever you go. Psalms 91:11-13 NLT

God asks Job...where were you, while the morning stars sang together and all the angels shouted for joy?

Job 38:7 NIV

Angels find their greatest joy praising God. Shouldn't we also?

They carry out God's plan. Luke 1:11-19

They carry out God's judgment. 2Samuel 24:16-17

They patrol the earth. Zechariah 1:10-11

They come to your aid and minister to you. Worship and praise God for this great plan of His.

I love you...Memaw

A Poured Out Spirit

Monday's Mediations: Seeking Him

As I seek to get closer to Jesus, I find one thing that helps and it is to have a speech that edifies. And this is what happens as I seek Jesus and live in Him.

And it shall come to pass afterward that I will pour out My Spirit on all flesh; your sons and daughters shall prophesy, your old men shall dream dreams, your young men shall see visions. And also, on My men servants and on My maid servants, I will pour out My Spirit in those days. Joel 2:28-29 KJV

Strive to get close to Jesus and receive His Spirit to live a life worth talking about.

I love you...Memaw

Good Morning Precious Children.

Tuesday's Tips: Glorious Is This Day

I know it's early and I know it's Tuesday, but God is still on the throne, and ALL is well with my soul.

What a glorious day our God has given us

Can you talk? Then praise God. Can you walk? Then rejoice. Can you hear? Then shout glory. Can you see? Then sing to the King who blessed you with HIS gift of sight. I tell you from His Word ALL your faculties, ALL your breath for your lungs is HIS gift from HIM to you. There is NO excuse to not be healed except unbelief. NONE. Jesus was beaten unrecognizable to give you, HIS gifts. He never even moaned from the pain of His beating, so He could give you the gift of healing. He, King Holy Jesus, without sin, was mutilated in His body to give you, His gift. Will you experience pain? Will you feel sick in your body? Sure, that's evil forces trying to take you out before you time. But God. Hallelujah, says here's My gift of healing put it on like a beautiful robe. So, I say get up from your aches and pains and tell The King Jesus how much you love Him and thank Him with the tongue He gave you to say it with.

Blessings with the gift of healing.... I love you...Memaw

Thank You Father God, for ALL my gifts from You. And EVERYBODY said Amen.

God's Goodness

Wednesday's Word: Your word

What do your words say about you? Does your word reveal blessings or grumblings to others? Does your word speak kindness or self-centeredness? Does your word encourage or criticize? Does your word take responsibility or blame others? What do your words say about you? Guess what God's Word says about Him and you. I personally believe that no one has ever been cursed at, worse than Jesus. But His Word says I love you. I forgive everything you have ever done. EVERYTHING.

God loves you so much that Pastor Chris says if God had a refrigerator, your picture would be on it. His Word speaks volumes about who He wants to be in your life. Savior, Lord, protector, healer, provider, shelter, comforter, teacher, deliverer, wisdom, understanding, kindness, love, joy, peace, long-suffering, gentle, and more than this text will hold. God is your ALL. Why would I want anything else? Or anyone else? Praise Him.

Because through Jesus I am His glory....Memaw

I love you, Jesus

In His Image

Thursday's Thoughts: What God Says He Means

As I awoke this morning as usual, the Holy Spirit began teaching me about the meaning of things in God's Word. And this is what He taught this morning. From Genesis 1:26...And God said (now when God speaks, you better pay close attention) "Let Us (meaning He, the Word and the Holy Spirit) make man (people) in Our image, after our likeness..." Awesome.

After many years as a believer in Christ, I learned that when God said He created us in His image, it meant He designed us to learn His characteristics and put them into practice in our lives. And that is true. But what God the Holy Spirit taught me this morning was God created us as a spirit just like Himself, Christ, and the Holy Spirit. But God covered our spirit with flesh. He gave us a will just like His. The only difference here is our wills can choose between doing the right things and doing sinful things. I believe the Holy Spirit was teaching me about being in His image, because of a conversation I had with my insurance company yesterday. I wanted them to explain why they took money out of our bank account for papa's truck that we had canceled.

Her explanation and my understanding didn't seem to be working together. And this young lady as I understood goes to church. But I could tell she wasn't happy with my questions, and at the end of our conversation, she sharply slammed her phone receiver down. This bothered me. So, I ask God what was happening, and this was my Holy Spirit answer. Your spirit recognized her spirit as not being in the image of God. Righteous spirits recognize the evil in people's spirits that are not like God's. Now think on this, if you are in Christ and your spirit is searching for the truth, the Holy Spirit will always teach you the truth.

Amen and Amen

By the love of Jesus...I love you...Memaw

Fruits To Live By

Friday's Fruit: If It Wasn't For The Fruit

Galatians 5:22-23 - But the Fruit of the Spirit is love, joy, peace, forbearance, kindness, goodness, faithfulness, gentleness. Against such things there is no law.

Did you get what the last seven words said? Against such things (our ways of living) there is no law (no command). When you receive Jesus and confess with your mouth Him as your Lord, He immediately gives you, in your spirit, that He created before the foundation of the world, and He also created you to live your fleshly life in His Spirit. When Jesus gave you His Spirit, His Spirit contains ALL this fruit. Now, through His Holy Spirit, you have the life of God living in you. Glory. So, if the Holy Spirit is given the right to live through you, then this Fruit is lived out of your life. You don't have to be commanded to love.

It just blows my mind to think or believe that I will live on this earth in God's image from His Holy Spirit in me. I don't even have to try to love others. The Holy Spirit loves them through me, which is true love, not fake or pretend love. So, what does your Fruit smell like to others? Is it perfect, or has it become rotten on the vine of your heart? You can test your fruit by what you think or say to others.

In Jesus' name...Amen

I love you Memaw.

Be Imitators Of God

Saturday's Sayings: Who Do You Imitate?

The Word of God is life, like no other. Ephesians 5...be imitators of God, ...walk in love...walk as children of light...learn what is pleasing to the Lord...understand what the will of the Lord is...always give thanks for ALL things in the name of our Lord Jesus...Ephesians 4...lay aside falsehood, speak truth to your neighbor...be kind to one another, tender hearted, forgiving each other, just as God in Christ has forgiven you.

Just saying from Jesus

I love you Memaw

Receive, Accept And Ask

Sunday's Song: Walk In Christ

There are three in God. God the Father, God the Son (Jesus), and God the Holy Spirit. There are three baptisms.

First baptism: Receive Jesus as your Lord and get water baptized.

Second: Accept the truth that Jesus is the only begotten Son of God, crucified and raised the third day again by the Holy Spirit. Then Jesus gives you the Holy Spirit. And you go to heaven one day.

Third: Ask God to give you His Holy Spirit, and He baptizes you with His Holy Spirit. This third baptism empowers you with the life of Christ in you that others recognize. Just being saved, as in the first step, you are going to heaven, but you don't have the power you need to WALK IN CHRIST. You are still in the world. Being baptized in the Holy Spirit means you are immersed in, not water, but Jesus and cannot be quiet around others about Him. Everything you do, every person you see knows about Jesus because He is your life now. Jesus lives through you. I can prove this. John 20:22 tells us Jesus breathed on His disciples before He ascended back to God. He did it because they truly believed that He was the Christ. But Acts 2:1 tells us that they were baptized with power and fire. Power to boldly talk about

Christ and fire to purify them from their old beliefs. Which life with Christ do you want? Just heaven-bound or power lived. As for me, I want power from Jesus' resurrection. The same Holy Spirit that raised Christ will raise me to power, freedom, deliverance and confidence, that Jesus is the Holy Living Son of God. More of Christ equals more presence of Him. I love you Jesus and I thank you for what you did for me so I can live for you.

Blessings favor joy forever...Memaw.

Godly Character

Monday's Meditations: Forbearance

Forbearance is a word found mostly in the King James Version of the Bible. It has two meanings. One is to delay repayment of a debt, as in "The borrowers request forbearance until they can provide the proper documents."

In the Bible, however, forbearance usually refers to a godly character trait. To forbear is to abstain or hold back; forbearance is similar to patience and self-control. Colossians 3:12–13 KJV is one example: "Put on therefore, as the elect of God, holy and beloved, bowels of mercies, kindness, humbleness of mind, meekness, longsuffering; Forbearing one another and forgiving one another." The New Living Translation words it this way: "Make allowance for each other's faults, and forgive anyone who offends you."

God shows forbearance in that He holds back the judgment the world deserves: "Or do you show contempt for the riches of his kindness, forbearance, and patience, not realizing that God's kindness and patience is intended to lead you to repentance?"
(Romans 2:4, KJV).

In this instance, forbearance refers to God's mercy, kindness, and longsuffering in delaying rightful judgment. Paul is warning mankind not to take God’s delay in dealing with sin as a sign that He is uninterested or that man is innocent. Paul warns people who think of themselves as so moral not to be hasty in judging others since God will judge everyone someday. The fact that God is so forbearing in judging the world, that it should cause us to forbear to judge others.

Are we so much better than God that we have the right NOT to forbear others?

I love you...Memaw.

Morning Precious Children

Tuesday's Tips: Savior

The Holy Spirit of God is so amazing and wonderful. That's the only words I can think of from my human mind to describe Him.

This morning, as I lay in bed after waking from my night's sleep, He began to talk. I love this time of my day. The beginning of it with God.

He said it's getting very close, talking about Christmas, to when we celebrate the time God chose to come live among man in the flesh. God came to earth and walked among us. He did it because that was the only way He could redeem man back to Himself. Little lambs could not do it. If God wanted to wipe out hurt, abuse, murder, and sin of all kinds, He would have had to wipe out all mankind again like in the days of Noah and start over.

But what would have happened to all those people. God would have lost them by not spending eternity with Him. And every time sin became rampant again, God would have had to wipe those out and start over again, and again, and again. It would have never stopped. But I love His plan. He came, God birthed Himself in flesh like the very ones He could have wiped out, just so we could live for Him now and with Him FOREVER. Can you see what life would have been if God had not become flesh to die for flesh so you would not have been wiped out? Whew what a glorious Almighty Father. A Father so loving of you that He chose flesh like yours to die so you would not be wiped out. I think our celebration of what an amazing Father we have should become a great worship instead of presents for each other. I know mine will be. Thank you, Father God and Holy Spirit, for sharing Jesus' life with me. Amen.

Love Memaw.

Morning The Upright In God

Wednesday's Word: Proverbs

(Pretend with me again, please)

Proverbs 16: NLT

Verse 16: How much better it is to get wisdom than gold

18...pride goes before destruction and a haughty spirit before stumbling

24...pleasant words are a honeycomb sweet to the soul and healing to the bones

28...a perverse man spreads strife and a slanderer separates intimate friends.

Proverbs 17: 4...An evildoer listens to wicked lips...
A liar pays attention to a destructive tongue.

From the Word of God...I love you Memaw

You Have Authority

Thursday's Thoughts: Your Focus

What you focus on becomes your life. If you focus more on your problems than on the truth of God's Word, you lose your strength to get out of the problem. Lean not on your own understanding but on Christ. Meditate, focus on God's Word and your problem goes away. The more you meditate on your problem the bigger your problem gets. Whatever you focus on becomes your calling. Whatever you focus on becomes your worship. Whatever you meditate on the most, becomes your power. You can't change your circumstances only God can when you let Him. Sometimes God allows the circumstances to change you. His Word will change your mind, heart, and focus. God has your answers.

You have not because you ask not. If you have a problem, go to God, not your friends. Again, you become what you focus on. If you focus on money problems, you have money problems. If you focus on what you don't have, you don't have it. If you focus on your sickness, you will be sick. What's your biggest focus? Is your focus on your problem or Jesus'? Whatever your focus is, that's what you have the most of.

Blessings, love and favor. I love you...Memaw.

Being Like Jesus

Friday's Fruit: Looking Like Jesus

But the fruit of the Spirit is love, joy, peace, forbearance, kindness, goodness, faithfulness, gentleness and self-control. Against such things there is no law." (Galatians 5:22-23)

The Greek word translated "fruit" refers to the natural product of a living thing. Paul used "fruit" to help us understand the product of the Holy Spirit, who lives inside every believer. The fruit of the Spirit is produced by the Spirit, not by the Christian. The Greek word is singular, showing that "fruit" is a unified whole, not independent characteristics. As we grow, all the characteristics of Christ will be manifested in our lives.

Yet, like physical fruit needs time to grow, the fruit of the Spirit will not ripen in our lives overnight. Like a successful gardener must battle against weeds to enjoy the sweet fruit they desire, we must constantly work to rid our lives of the "weeds" of our old sinful natures that want to choke out the work of the Spirit.

The Holy Spirit gives us the power we need to reject those old sinful desires. We can say "no" to sin and accept the "way out" that God faithfully provides by following the Holy Spirit's leading. (1 Corinthians 10:13)

As we give the Spirit more control of our lives, He begins to do in and through us what only He can do - to shape us and grow us to look like Jesus.

(2 Corinthians 3:17-18).

Since God's goal for all His children is for us to be like Jesus (Romans 8:29), the Holy Spirit constantly works to rid our lives of the "acts of the sinful nature" and display His fruit instead. (Gal 5:19) Therefore, the presence of the "fruit of the Spirit" is evidence that our character is becoming more like Christ's.

Heaven has a culture and you should live it out, if you don't you have lost your flavor.

I love you Memaw and Jesus

Jesus King Of Your Life.

Saturday's Sayings: Who Is King Of Your Life?

King: a man who holds by life tenure, and usually by hereditary right, the chief authority over a country and people. God or Christ, a person or THING preeminent in its class.

This beautiful journey that God has provided for me and papa in our move to Daphne is amazing. But with all the beauty, comfort, peace, and excitement of our new place, I never want it to become King of my life. Nothing I possess on earth can I take with me into eternity to be with Jesus. I am grateful, I am so blessed, I am humbled at what God has provided me and papa here. But again, none of this is for eternity. The only thing that I have, that I can take into eternity is my salvation, any deeds I did for Christ, and those souls I told about Jesus. That's why only He should be King of my life. Ask yourself, what would make me upset if I lost it? I pray it's not stuff. Examine your life. What is your King, or who is your King? The definition says kings can be people or things we value most.

But seek first his kingdom and his righteousness, and all these things will be given to you as well.

Matthew 6:33

Blessings...love and peace I give you and not stuff...Memaw

Is Jesus Your Praise?

Sunday's Song: JESUS None Other

Do people see Jesus in you?

If Christ Jesus is not glorified through you why even know Him?

My every breath He gave me to take to keep living in this body should shout GLORY to Jesus.

If I live for any other reason than Jesus, I have nothing of value to live for.

If Jesus is not PRAISED with my life, then life amounts to nothing in the end.

2 Corinthians 3:18 NIV- and we who with unveiled faces all REFLECT the Lord's glory are being transformed into His likeness with ever increasing glory which comes from the Lord who is the Spirit.

If your face is veiled (covered) with things of this life you can't reflect the life of Christ in you to others.

Blessings from Jesus...love you Memaw

The Power Of God.

Monday's Meditations: The Word Of God Is Not Void Of Power

Ephesians 3:20 KJV - Now unto him that is able to do exceedingly abundantly above all that we ask or think, according to the power that worketh in us,

According to the power within you. There are laws that govern faith. A relationship with God is the key to my miracle. In the beginning was the Word. The Word is the beginning of your answer. The Word is the beginning of your healing. The Word is the beginning of your salvation. The Word is the beginning of your life. The Word is the beginning of everything you want or need in and from the kingdom.

Want something, need something to happen that you know is what God wants for you? The Word is your answer.

Until you go to the Word for what you want God to do, you may never receive what you want.

Peace makers. Are you willing to make the changes in order to have peace? Want peace? Determine in your heart to have it.

1PETER 3:11 NIV: They must turn from evil and do good; they must seek peace and pursue it.

Remember Jesus is the prince of peace.

I love you...Memaw

Tuesday's Tips: It's Your Choice

Ephesians 3:17-19 NKJV....that Christ may dwell in your hearts through faith; that you, being rooted and grounded in LOVE, may be able to comprehend with all the saints.... the love of Christ which passes knowledge.

Does Christ dwell in your heart? Dwell means to live. Do you understand how much Jesus loves you? If Jesus lives in your heart, then He should be reflected to others. Other people should see Him in you. He lives in your heart by you believing that He lives in you.

Your confidence that Christ lives in you will bring about such a love from you that people will be drawn to Jesus through you.

You have to decide who you want people to see, you or Christ. Jesus will not overpower your decision. If you don't choose to give Him place or position in you life, He want be visible in you. The decision is who is the most important to you. Trying to look and act like Jesus only muddies the truth. It's either you or Him in you. It can never be both.

Blessings from Jesus and Memaw...I love you

Love Bears All Things

Wednesday's Word: What Do You Believe

The old saying, "what you see is what you get." The Word of God says what you believe is what you get.

John 3:15-17 KJ V

That whosoever believeth in him should not perish, but have eternal life

Mark 11:24 KJV

Therefore I say to you, whatever things you ask when you pray, believe that you receive them, and you will have them.

Matthew 21:22 KJV

And all things, whatsoever ye shall ask in prayer, believing, ye shall receive.

So I guess it's true, what you believe is what you get?

1CORITHIANS 13: 7 ESV says:

Love bears all things, believes all things, hopes all things, endures all things.

Enjoy your Fruit of LOVE along with believing God's Word and you will be amazingly joyful. I believe...and love you...Memaw

Standards, Commands And Precepts

Thursday's Thought: Who Sets Your Standards?

God has set standards, commands, precepts, and ordinances for His people. God says He is your strength. But if you don't live by His standards, He can't give you His strength to overcome the battle. You can't live by your own standards or the world's and expect God to give you His strength to live those standards. God is your strength when you live by His standards. Doing the same thing over and over that never changes your circumstance is not following God's Word. If your circumstances never change, maybe you need to do something different. You can't expect God to change your circumstances if you keep living in them or always going back to them. Think about where you are in your life. Is your life full of joy and peace? If you don't have joy and peace, it's not God's fault. Stop doing or allowing the same thing to happen, apply God's standards, and He will see to it that things change in your life.

I love you, Jesus, and thank you for loving me.

I love you, children...Memaw.

Friday's Fruit: What's Your Attitude?

Matthew 5:3 NIV...Blessed are the poor in spirit, for theirs is the kingdom of heaven.

Some time ago, I asked you, "who set your standards?" Or who determines how you live...how do you respond to certain situations...or how do you act because of what they did? How do you live when you are hurt...disappointed...and heartbroken? How do you respond when criticized...mocked...and made fun of or when someone reminds you of a stupid thing you did years ago that you are ashamed of now? How do I act or react to hateful remarks or ridiculing comments about a decision I made to live a godlier life?

Well, God gave me a picture this morning about Pontus Pilate making his soldiers hang a sign over the top of the cross that Jesus was crucified on saying...King of the Jews. The sign was correct, but Pilate put it there to insult the Jews.

What comment has someone made about you that was true but said it to insult you...mock you? They were trying to hurt you or disgrace you in public. When this happens take your foot and draw a blood line...the blood line of Jesus. Daring Satan to cross over His blood to destroy you. He will nitpick you, but he can't cross the bloodline of Christ to get to you. Draw the blood line of Jesus over yourself...your home...your family...your work...your travels...your decisions. Nothing can cross that bloodline unless you let them. The buck stops at the bloodline. When people criticize ... condemn ... and shame you, it's Satan using them. Forgive them.

Forgiving them is not for them...it's for you. Poor in spirit means you have a need for God. And when you get Him, He gives you, His kingdom.

WOW.

So, you decide what you want...worlds stuff or kingdom stuff.

Last tip: don't try and force your standards on others. Your standards will never fit them because they are yours.

Holy Spirit, bless the work and words of my children.

Amen

I love you...Memaw.

Forever Loved

Saturday's Sayings: Are You Loved?

God says: For God so (much) loved the world, that He gave His only beloved Son. He gave His Word, God can't break His Word. He took Word and made it flesh so He could die to take away my sins, nasty actions, harmful responses. God says that's who I am. Love. God is love, so He could not be any different. If you feel like you are not loved, well maybe not by the people you would like to love you, but NEVER lose the fact God loves you no matter where you are in your life. God still loves you. Even when I acted nastily, He still loved me. You may have a hard time getting that in your mind but that doesn't change the fact that God loves you because that's who our Father is. I love every one of you, but my love will never be able to give you eternal life. And nothing going on in your life here will go with you into eternity.

Wow. All this stuff won't be there. Now ain't that love.

Grace...Memaw

Believe - Receive

Sunday's Song: Making A Mountain Our Of A Mole Hill

Praise Jesus, from whom ALL blessings come to you.

Mark 11:23-25 The Message Bible

Jesus says as a matter of fact: "Embrace this God-life. Really embrace it, and nothing will be too much for you. This mountain, for instance: Just say, 'Go jump in the lake'—no shuffling or hemming and hawing—and it's as good as done. That's why I urge you to pray for absolutely everything, ranging from small to large. Include everything as you embrace this God-life, and you'll get God's everything. And when you assume the posture of prayer, remember that it's not all about asking. If you have anything against someone, forgive—only then will your heavenly Father be inclined to also wipe your slate clean of sins."

Now ain't that simple? If Jesus was on earth today, would He not just ask the Father for anything and believe that the Father would grant His request? Yep. Just that simple. And He says in Mark 11:23-25 you can do it to. Ask and believe God does it and it's done. But if you are not sure then don't expect God to give you what you ask Him for. Know without an ounce of doubt that God will answer and He has to because He said He would and He NEVER goes back on His Word.

NEVER.

We don't get our requests answered because we don't believe God will do it.

Believe ALL things from God, receive ALL things. Amen

I believe I received when I prayed. And the mountains disappear. Memaw

Morning Children. I Love You

Monday's Meditations: Praising Jesus

I will praise the Lord no matter what happens. I will constantly speak of His glories and grace. Psalms 34:1 TLB

Thank you, Jesus, for Your awesome love. Thank you, Holy Spirit, for God's guidance and protection. Thank You, Father for my life.

I will instruct you, says the Lord, and guide you along the best pathway for your life. Psalms 32:8 TLB

How precious is Your constant love, O Lord. Psalms 36:7a TLB

Bless the reading of Your Word O Lord God. That each one in this family believes with all their heart every word You speak. Amen and amen.

For His praise...Memaw

Compromising?

Tuesday's Tips: Compromise: impaired or diminished in function - weakened - damaged.

Thank You, Father, for these amazing children You have given me. In Jesus' name. AMEN

God does not condone or put up with compromising His commands.

Daniel 1:8-14...Daniel worked out a comprise with the Babylonians. What he did was work out a solution to whether or not they could eat Babylonian foods.

Compromise is a basic skill in marriage. Where keeping peace is more important than getting your way. But when it comes to God's commands, Deuteronomy 5:33 NIV- be careful to do what the Lord your God has commanded you, do not turn aside to the right or to the left.

Psalms 119:3 NLT - joyful are those who do not comprise with evil and they walk only in His paths. God is holy...and His ways are right. God is good...and His ways are life-giving.

What God says we will not negotiate...bargain...or compromise.

As we go through life, we will hear many calls to compromise...the fleeting pleasures of sin Hebrews 11:25

Hollow and deceptive philosophy Colossians 2:8

The lust of the flesh...the lust of the eyes...and the pride of life 1JOHN 2:16 NIV

We would never think about tossing Jesus aside for an idol. But compromise says we can have our idol and keep Jesus too.

Learn to know when compromise is appropriate and when it's not.

We can compromise on preferences but not on principles. Ask: will my compromise hurt or help...will it be right or wrong?

More of HIM less of me...Memaw

Expecting

Wednesday's Word: Are You Expecting From God?

Psalms 1:6 TLB... For the Lord watches over all the plans and paths of the godly....

Psalms 8:10 TLB...All those who know Your mercy, Lord, will COUNT on You for help, for You have never yet forsaken those who trust in You.

God is expecting you to count on Him.

Psalms 18:30 TLB...What a God He is! How perfect in every way! ALL HIS promises prove true. He is a shield for everyone who hides behind Him.

I love HIS Word. And walk in His statues...Memaw

Blessed

Thursday's Thoughts: Blessed Are His Standards

Why would I expect God to bless something if my whole heart was not in it?

God died in flesh so He could give us His best.

Don't be surprised if some people won't have anything to do with you because you set your standards as God's standards.

Unless you ask God to forgive you and you forgive others, you will always be miserable.

Being forgiven by Jesus does not make me better than others, it just makes me better than who I used to be.

It's impossible to live by God's standards unless we live by the fruit of the Holy Spirit.

Blessing's children...I love you Memaw.

Morning Children Of His Peace

Friday’s Fruit: Peace

And the peace of God, which transcends all understanding, will guard your hearts and your minds in Christ Jesus.

Philippians 4:7 NIV

But if you don't guard your mind from the things of the world, it's impossible for God to give you peace.

Knowing Jesus, knowing His Word that tells you what He promises you will be the source of true life. True peace.

In the name of Jesus, I speak peace over you today.

I love you...Memaw

Your Inheritance

Saturday's Sayings: Are You Satisfied With Jesus?

Let's pretend, you have a great, great, great uncle. You just received a letter in the mail from his lawyer who has been given the authority to administer all the wealth when he died and left his entire estate to you. The letter indicated that your uncle had a lot of wealth and possessions. What are you going to do with your new estate? Are you going to take all of it and live it up? Drinking, buying drinks for your friends, buying everything you see? What will you do with your newfound wealth?

Now let's look at this story through the eyes of the Bible. Your great, great, great uncle is God. He owns everything, all the cattle on a thousand hills, and when you RECEIVE God's Son Jesus, as your PERSONAL Lord, then He becomes your advocate (lawyer) who has been given the authority to administer God's possessions to you. The letter you received is the Bible. It holds all your inherited wealth. So now what are you doing with your new wealth? It's yours through Jesus. Are you asking for anything you have inherited? Have you read the estate letter and found what you have inherited? Are you going to find out what you have inherited or are you going to sit in poverty and whine about not having anything? If you want to know how to possess your inheritance, ask for wisdom. Want eternal life? Accept Christ as your Lord. Want what you inherited ask God in Jesus' name and believe it's yours and you get it. Want to be healed every time sickness or affliction hits you? Receive it by believing it's yours and rebuke the one who is trying to make you sick. You can't get sick and stay sick unless you receive it when Satan throws it at you. Tell him no get out I inherited healing in Jesus' name.

Open your Bible and find out what you inherited.

I love you, and bless you, Jesus. And I love you, and bless you, children, Memaw

God Has His Hand On You

Sunday's Song: Whose Hand Is On You?

Exodus 3:19-20 KJV...And I am sure that the king of Egypt will not let you go, unless a mighty hand compels him. And I will stretch out My hand and smite Egypt with all My wonders which I will do in the midst thereof: and after that he will let you go.

Again, who's hand is on you? I declare to you today in the name of Jesus that the mighty hand of God is on you.

Now, if the hand of pharaoh called hurt, failure, disappointment, discouragement, anxiety, worry, fear, sickness, finances or anything that seems like you will never get through, then take a deep breath because there is a mighty hand called the love of Jesus that is compelled to let it go. Whatever your King of Egypt is, the hand of God is mightier. And He is compelled to help you. But as Moses had to do you will have to do what God has told you to do so He will make your Pharaoh, let go of you.

Beautiful. Reread this scripture again and believe that God has His hand on you.

I love you...Memaw

His Word Is Life

Monday's Meditations: What's In Your Hand?

Moses had a staff in his hand. Exodus 4:2 ... the Lord said unto him, what is that in thine hand? And he said, "A rod." And He said, "Cast it on the ground." And he cast it on the ground, and it became a serpent; and Moses fled from before it.

Forty years earlier, Moses had killed the Egyptian with his hand. Before Moses met the Lord God in the wilderness tending his father-in-law's sheep, Moses still had that day back in Egypt on his hands.

Something he was not proud of. Something he did to another person. Something his friends knew what he had done. What's in your hand? Is it something in your life you are sorry for, or is there something you are still holding in your hand, something that someone did to you that still hurts?

God asked Moses a few verses later to throw what was in his hand (staff) (his past life). And his (staff) his past life became a snake. Is that what your past looks like, a venomous snake that at any moment can come back to bite you?

We have two hands. One hand is our good hand; the hand we let everyone see. Then we have a withered hand, the hand we hide so no one will see our other life.

The withered hand that has anger, hurt, fear, disappointment, and past mistakes in it. But God said give me your hand, the hand that has something in it that I can restore.

God said tell my people that My Name is I AM.

Read His Word. I love you Memaw

Tuesday's Tips: Faithfulness

Who Or What Is Your Faithfulness To?

Being faithful in little things will cause God to bless you with greater things. What about being faithful with what God has provided for you? Do you own a car or truck? Would you walk to work or the store instead of driving your vehicle? Do you have a house? Would you sleep in a tent instead of your home? I believe your answer would be "no" to these questions. Then why would we not use the gifts God has provided us in our daily life? What about your finances? Do you spend wisely and give generously? If you do, are you faithful? If you are the glory of Christ, as God's Word says you are, are you giving God back His glory from your life? You have to know in your heart that you are His Glory before you can give it back to Him. What about your salvation? How do you use it in your daily life? And lastly, what do you do with your spiritual gifts? Are you ministering to those who need your gifts?

Hum...lot of questions. Using what God provides is being faithful to Him. Blessings, peace, grace, and joy in the Lord.

I love you...Memaw

The Favor Of God

Wednesday's Word: Favored

What God favors He empowers. For You, Lord, will bless the righteous; with favor will You surround us as with a shield. Psalms 5:12 KJV

Let us in all our seeking see that we have the favor of God. Keep His commandments. Walk in the Spirit. Be tender hearted and lovable. If we do these things, our ministry will be a blessing to others.

You are my favorite...I love you...Memaw

Thursday's Thoughts: Is God Enough For You?

God is more eager to answer than we are to ask.

How bountiful is God when we depend on Him? He even gives us enough to share with others.

I love you...Memaw

It Is Finished

Friday's Fruit: What's your IT?

Mark 9:22 NIV..."It" has often thrown him into fire or water to kill him. But if you can do anything, take pity on us and help us.

One time, correction, many times I have gotten angry with someone and said, "You are so dumb." I looked and saw the color drain from their face. After a moment they said...can you at least say something about what I did, and not who I am. In other words, say something about my "it" and not about me.

Can you name all the dumb, stupid, shameful things you did?

Now name all the things Jesus did for you.

If you can't hear the Word, you can't speak it.

Next time you go to God in prayer, don't bring Him your problem, your "it." Bring Him you. You're not an "it" you are the one God gave me.

Remember, Jesus said "It" Is Finished.

Just some tips from Jesus...and Memaw. I love you

The Risen Christ

Saturday's Sayings: Where Do You Go After The Mountain Top?

Mark 9. Jesus was on the mountain where He was transformed to spend a few moments with God His Father, Moses, and Elijah. When His visit with His Father was over, He, along with Peter, James, and John, came down the mountain to find His disciples arguing with the experts of the law.

Is this what happens to you on your way down the mountain? People start making snide remarks about you and your journey with Jesus.

Notice in verse 24 the boy's father said he did believe but wanted Jesus to help him with the part of his belief that he was having trouble with. The father didn't lose his faith. He just didn't look in the right place for it.

When your faith seems weak, just go look at where you last had it. Look under and in the places that your faith was last known to be. You never lose your faith; it just sometimes gets misplaced.

I love you and bless you, Memaw

Do You Believe?

Sunday’s Song: What's On Your Thoughts?

Mark 5:25-34 tells us the story of a woman with an issue of blood. Scripture says she had this sickness for 12 years. And had spent her entire bank account on doctors trying to get well. After 12 years, she was no better; in fact her condition was worse. But she THOUGHT if I could just touch the hem of Jesus' garment, she believed she would be made well.

What do you think about when you have a problem? If you're like me you think of 10,000 things to see if you can fix your situation. But the thought that you act on is usually the one that fixes it, solves it, or heals it.

Thoughts get you nowhere. But acting on the thoughts that you BELIEVE will change the circumstances for the better, is the one that usually works. This woman in Mark thought and believed that what she could do would heal her, and she acted on her thought. Acting on your thoughts does something. But some thoughts can get you in trouble. If your thoughts you act on bring about good things, go for it. But if your actions are from thoughts just to get even, then look out for the consequences that will make your situation worse.

Just thinking about you, Jesus and Memaw and we both have thoughts for the best for you. I love you

Waste Nothing

Monday's Meditations: No Regrets

Jesus said, "Have the people sit down." There was plenty of grass in that place, and they sat down (about five thousand men were there). Jesus then took the loaves, gave thanks, and distributed to those who were seated as much as they wanted. He did the same with the fish.

When they had all had enough to eat, he said to his disciples, "Gather the pieces that are left over. Let nothing be wasted." So, they gathered them and filled twelve baskets with the pieces of the five barley loaves left over by those who had eaten.
John 6:10-13

What did these verses say to you?

This is how Jesus, through the Holy Spirit's work, explained it to me. At the beginning of your salvation life, you only have a small amount of a relationship with Jesus, God, and the Holy Spirit. But after Jesus breaks His Word open to you, and over time, and until the end of your life, there will be something of Him in you leftover to leave others.

During your journey with Christ many people should have been fed. He also said, "waste nothing" about Him.

You have less than a second to get it right - don't let that second cause you to regret.

Blessings and favor...with love...Memaw

Tuesday's Tips: Train Up A Child In The Way He Should Go, And When He Is Old, He Will Not Depart.

Proverbs 22:6

I had a beautiful teaching from the Holy Spirit on this scripture this morning. I believed this verse meant I was to be taught, and I was to teach my children what I had learned. I if I teach them about God, it would help them stay straight. Well, that teaching didn't work on me. So, I figured I apparently wasn't a good learner when it came to God and His Word because I couldn't seem to ever do the right thing.

So, this morning the Holy Spirit put it on my heart to research this verse in the Greek and Hebrew languages. And here is what I found.

Train or train up...to nurture, dedicate, educate, instruct in practical knowledge.

Ok. Sounds good. Sweet children, what I learned was the parents are to train, educate, (look out here comes preaching, and do not use the TV to teach them because we're too busy).

Ouch. Forgive me and keep reading.

Next, “in the way he should go.” This means instruct him/her in what and how he needs to learn about life and God. Not instructed to be like his sister or brother. Like his way. When you try to make a child learn to live like someone else, it doesn’t work. He/she wasn't designed to be like someone else. This teaching confuses him/her. Later in life, he doesn't know how to live. The scripture says "the way he should go" not your way. This also doesn't mean you give him free rein to choose his path because flesh will choose wrong things almost every time. Teach him in his design, and he will stay with it even in old age. He chooses his path in life by his design and great instruction from his parents.

Warning: he gets to choose his path in life, not gender. Blessed will be the parents who learn and do this. The rest of us just have to be forgiven.

I love you and am so blessed by you.

And my side note: You are all, in my view, doing a great job training your children. Just wanted to teach you something I didn't know.

Memaw and Jesus

Rejoice Always

Wednesday's Word: Singing, Even In The Rain

What's your song? Or should I say how does your song go?

What tune forms your song?

What are your lyrics?

Is your song grateful or discouraged?

Your song comes from the person inside your soul. Your soul controls or houses your will. Those things you are determined to do or not do. Soul makes your choices and decisions for life. Your soul displays your emotions, hurts, anger, sadness, happiness, and disappointment. Your soul, guided by your heart and mind, determines everything you do. Your choices are set in motion in your soul. With ALL these parts soul, mind and heart bring forth your song.

But again, you are the one who makes the choice of what your song is about. Even if your circumstances came from another person's decisions you still have a choice as to how you sing your song. And I can guarantee, that if you daily, or 10,000 times a day, sing songs of praise, your soul will fall in line with it. Your soul will not be bothered with the questions and concerns of your situation. Yes, your problem will still have to be addressed but your song of praise will determine how you go through your problem.

I have a suggestion. Start your song with, "Oh.... how I love Jesus, oh.... how I love Jesus, oh.... how I love Jesus...because He first loved me " .... awesome now sing it again...but louder this time.

Now sing.

My Jesus and Memaw love me. My Jesus and Memaw love me. My Jesus and Memaw love me because she loves God and is loved by Him.

As Papa says, “sing it out, Billy Byrd.”

I love you and bless you, today. Memaw

Faith

Thursday's Thoughts: Faith Without Works Is Dead Faith

You don't have to come to me to make your request known to God, because you have access to God through Jesus.

You can't move forward without a dream.

The answer to your question is within you...it's the Holy Spirit.

Do you have an AMEN faith? Or an earthly amen? Think about it. Do you say amen because of habit, or do you say AMEN because you believe in God for the request you made to Him?

I love you Memaw

Friday's Fruit: Always

Rejoice in the Lord ALWAYS (not when everything is going well) ALWAYS. Again, I will say REJOICE Philippines 4:4 NIV

You can't be bothered by something and Rejoice at the same time.

This verse goes on to say...Let your gentle spirit be known to all men.

Today I ask Jesus to bless each of you with favor before ALL men.

I love you...Memaw

From Ashes To Beauty

Saturday's Sayings: Got Any Problems, Hurts, Or Disappointments?

Provide for those who grieve to bestow on them a crown of beauty instead of ashes, the oil of joy instead of mourning, and a garment of praise instead of a spirit of despair. They will be called oaks of righteousness, a planting of the LORD for the display of his splendor."

– ISAIAH 61:3 NIV

Thank You, Lord, for ALL Your promises. Only when we believe Your promises are true and are ours, when we see ashes turn to beauty. Oils of joy. And a garment life that praises You. Then we will see the display of Your splendor. I love You, Jesus. I thank You for Your love for me. I praise You that my life doesn't have to always be ashes and that You are the one that will turn my ashes into beauty. But I have to let go of my ashes for You to give me my beautiful life.

AMEN

I love you beautiful children...Memaw

Morning Amazing children.

Sunday's Song: Who Are You?

Jesus Christ came to earth as God in the flesh, just to teach us how to live as God desired us to live for Him in the flesh.

Are you in the world or are you in Christ?

Therefore, if anyone is in Christ, he is a new creation. The old has passed away; behold, the new has come.
2CORITHIANS 5:18 KJV

Beautiful...I love you...Memaw

Morning Restored For God.

Monday's Meditations: Restoration and Payback

And I will restore to you the years that the locust hath eaten, the cankerworm, and the caterpillar; and the palmerworm, my great army which I sent among you. Joel 2:25 KJV

What is particularly significant about this verse in Joel is the fact that it speaks of a season of decrease and decay in terms of years, meaning it was a long, arduous season.

Sometimes when there are areas that we have dealt with for a long time, such as ongoing health issues, a lengthy season of insufficient financial supply, or a drawn-out family struggle, we can fall into the repetitive cycle of that season until we can't see anything different. Often under such circumstances, we can begin to tolerate what is and not expect a time of restoration to ever emerge. It's time to expect that God will take that long season and restore everything that was lost during it. Change your expectations today and know that restoration and payback are upon you.

Love it, believe it, or it will never happen. I love you...Memaw

Morning Grateful Children

Tuesday's Tips: Today's Motivation

Accept opposition as proof of your progress.

Spiritual warfare always surrounds the birth of a miracle.

Nothing is ever as bad as it first appears.

Battle is the opportunity to prove what you believe.

Joseph proved that opposition is the wave that takes you from the pit to the palace.

The size of your enemy determines the size of your reward.

Do not let any enemy decide the timing of battle, nor the weapons you will use.

Devotional from MJ's Sunday night small group

I love each of you...Memaw

Pondering

Wednesday's Word: What Are You "Pondering " In Your Heart?

But Mary kept all these things and pondered them in her heart. Luke 2:19 NKJV

To ponder is to weigh in the mind: to think about, reflect on, to think or consider especially quietly, soberly, and deeply.

You will not live an obedient life with a closed Bible.

Now ponder that.

Are you partially or fully obedient to the Word of God?

Partial obedience will not get your prayers answered.
Humm.

I ponder how much I love every one of you. Memaw

Gratitude And Disposition

Thursday's Thoughts: What Is Your Attitude?

Gratitude: being thankful; a readiness to show appreciation for and to return kindness.

Disposition: A person's inherent qualities and character, unusual attitude of one's spirit, outlook, mood, and attitude.

When God brought these two words to my mind this week, I wondered why. And in my quiet time before daylight, He caused me to reflect on both of these words in my own life. As I thought about my gratitude, God gave me a picture of the stories I have heard or read about. Stories of people who didn't have food unless they went to the local garbage dump. The only clothes they had, came from dumpster piles. Some only had roofs over them at night from cardboard, being held up by poles from dead trees they found along the road. One man was seen carrying about a 15–20-foot dead tree down the road. When the visitor to that country saw it, he asked his guide the reason. He was told that the dead tree was valuable. He could sell it to buy food for his family.

Ephesians 2:7...Now God has us where he wants us, with all the time in this world and the next to shower grace and kindness upon us in Christ Jesus. Saving is all his idea, and all his work. All we do is trust him enough to let him do it. It's God's gift from start to finish! We don't play the major role. If we did, we'd probably go around bragging that we'd done the whole thing!

Now do you understand why you are living where you are? God put you here to save you and protect you from what others have to endure. Maybe you would be more grateful if you had to get up every morning and go to the garbage dump for your day's meal.

Now what about your disposition? How do you truly feel about what you have?

"God said, they have nothing and rejoice. You have everything and you complain, grip and even disrespect what I have blessed you with. What you have is my gift to you because I want to bless you."

WOW.

I love you Memaw

Faith Established

Friday's Fruit: Reach Out In Your Faith.

Jesus said to him, if you can believe, all things are possible to him who believes. Mark 9:23 NKJV

ALL things are possible in what you believe. Even if you don't believe the truth of God's Word, you still believe that it's not true.

Whatever you decide IS what you believe.

Desire God, and you will have desires from Him.

When God drops something in your heart, it's because there is a purpose for it. It's something He intends to carry out to completion.

Watch out, the enemy is all about trying to stop you. Resist the urge to abandon what God has appointed for you to do.

God has established you, and He will see you through. Just believe.
Just Jesus.

I love you...... Memaw

A Great And Mighty God

Saturday's Sayings: Psalms 41:1-3 TLB

God blesses those who are kind to the poor. He helps them out of their troubles. He protects them and keeps them alive; He publicly honors them and destroys the power of their enemies. He nurses them when they are sick and soothes their pains and worries.

AMEN

I love you dearly...Memaw

Think On These Things

Sunday's Song: Think!

Praying in the name of Jesus...are your prayers legitimate or illegitimate?

You use Jesus' name because you have authority from God.

God never turns down Jesus.

You call Me Lord, Lord...but don't do what I say.

What is God going to get out of answering your prayers?

The time between your request and God's answer is preparation. Preparing the answer for you and preparing you for the answer. Sweet.

I love you in Jesus' name...I have His authority. Memaw

Trusting Him

Monday's Meditations: Selfish or Self-less

Notes from a message.

You cannot be happy and selfish at the same time.

You cannot trust a person to always take care of you. Trust God, and He will always take care of you.

If you are truly walking in love, you won't have all the problems you have.

People can tell the difference between true love and fake.

God says don't ask me to help someone that you can do yourself.

ALL of us at some time or other have a mountain. The problem is, do we keep going around the same mountain?

Jesus is coming soon...be ready.

I love you...Memaw

Taking Jesus At His Word

Tuesday's Tips: We Ae His Life. What Have We Done With It?

And He saw two boats lying at the edge of the lake; but the fishermen had gotten out of them and were washing

their nets. And he entered into one of the ships, which was Simon's, and prayed him, that he would thrust out a little from the land. And he sat down and taught the people out of the ship.

Now, when he had left speaking, he said unto Simon, "Launch out into the deep, and let down your nets for a draught." Luke 5:2-4

The disciples were washing their nets because they had given up. They had failed, they had lost their direction, they had lost their belief, they had lost their desire.

Have you?

BUT Jesus said throw your nets into the deep.

What God has for you is in the deep.

My biggest regret is that I didn't go deeper. I didn't go deep because things were safe, comfortable. But look at what I left in the deep because I wouldn't go there.

Nevertheless, at God's Word it shall come to pass. Stop washing your nets, God is not through with you.

Glory. Hallelujah.

Listen, God is not through with you. Forget about your nets. Failures, lost time, disappointments, mistakes and sins. Through His blood we are His life.

I love you...Memaw

New Creation

Wednesday's Word: Are You In Or Out?

The reason we are not who we are supposed to be is because we want Christ to be us instead of us, being Christ.

2CORITHIANS 5:17 – NIV

Therefore, if anyone is in Christ, the new creation has come: The old has gone, the new is here!

Blessings...find out who you are and who you want to be...Memaw

Sacred Covenant

Thursday's Thoughts: What's In Your Marriage?

Your marriage is a mission, not a means of someone taking care of your wants.

A good marriage is not a contract between a man and a woman, but rather, a sacred covenant between three; the man, the woman and God.

Ephesians 5:31-32 KJV- "For this cause shall a man leave his father and mother, and shall be joined unto his wife, and they two shall be one flesh.

Have you become married, one with Christ, or have you walked away from Him for something you think is better for you?

Be careful or you will wind up in bed with Satan.

Grace...Memaw

News Flash

Friday's Fruit: Breaking News

Are you a follower of Jesus? You follow what is most important to you.

Walk in obedience to all that the Lord your God has commanded you, so that you may live and prosper and prolong your days in the land that you will possess.
Deuteronomy 5:33 NIV

The Lord Himself goes before you and will be with you; He will never leave you nor forsake you. Do not be afraid; do not be discouraged. Deuteronomy 31:8 NIV

Direct my footsteps according to Your Word;
Let no sin rule over me. Psalm 119:133 NIV

It is the Lord your God you must follow, and Him you must revere. Keep His commands and obey Him; serve Him and hold fast to Him. Deuteronomy 13:4 NIV

Then He called the crowd to Him along with His disciples and said: "Whoever wants to be My disciple must deny themselves and take up their cross and follow Me." Mark 8:34 NIV

Unload the world and follow Him....Memaw

A Servant To All

Saturday's Sayings: What's Your Life Like?

Are you a Saul life or are you a Paul life?

Saul hurt, hunted down, and killed those he didn't agree with.

And I was in complete agreement when your witness Stephen was killed. I stood by and kept the coats they took off when they stoned him. Acts 20:22 NLT

Meanwhile, Saul was still breathing out murderous threats against the Lord's disciples. He went to the high priest and asked him for letters to carry to the synagogues in Damascus, so that if he found any there who belonged to the Way, whether men or women, he might take them as prisoners to Jerusalem. Acts 9:1-3 NIV

But when Saul, became Paul he loved, sought out, encouraged, and brought the eternal life of Christ to those that didn't agree with Christ.

For though I am free from all men, I have made myself a servant to all, that I might win more of them. To the Jews I became as a Jew, in order to win Jews. To those under the law I became as one under the law (though not being myself under the law) that I might win those under the law.

1 Corinthians 9:19–23 NKJV

Which life are you?

Because I love you...Memaw

Sold Out

Sunday's Song: What Do You Have For Sale?

Are you having trials, troubles, and persecution? Is it because you have sold the right decision, for the wrong one?

If you are being persecuted it's either a wrong choice, or it's because you are standing firm in Christ.

If you are not being persecuted, it's because you are going in the same direction as Satan. You only bump into things when you're going in the opposite direction.

If you're standing for Christ, you are going to bump into Satan.

If you truly understand what Jesus went through for you and your salvation, it would NEVER be for sale. You would never exchange it for something in this world.

For God so loved you...He gave and never sold out.

I love you, Memaw.

One more fruit. If you're not being persecuted, it's because people don't know you are a Christian.

Following Who You Favor

Monday’s Meditations: Who's Your Favorite?

You will never be happy while everything is about you. You are only happy when it's about Jesus and others.

When did Jesus become not enough for you?

The enemy is trying to take away the agreement you made as a married couple. He wants to tear you apart so you won't have the home you should have.

John 10:10 (ASV) The thief cometh not, but that he may steal, and kill, and destroy. I came that they may have life and may have [it] abundantly.

You follow who you favor...love and blessing Memaw

I Have Called You

Tuesday's Tips: Where Are You Supposed To Go?

If God has called you and not those around you, go.

God will not lead you into something that will harm you.

What harms you is disobedience to His call.

Don't let the world, friends, or family tell you who you are. God formed you before the foundation of the world. He already knew who you were.

But now thus says the Lord, He who created you, O Jacob, He who formed you, O Israel: "Fear not, for I have redeemed you; I have called you by name, you are Mine. Isaiah 43:1

Could not have said it better myself.

Love you Memaw

Cock A Doodle Do

Wednesday's Word: Have You Heard The Rooster Crow?

All sins committed by a believer in Jesus are an act of betrayal.

Peter betrayed Jesus by denying Him three times.

Hearing your rooster crow is the process by which you realize you have sinned and you are broken-hearted about it

.

What kind of past do you have? Guess what, all of Jesus' disciples had a past they were sorry for. But God still used them mightily.

EVERY DAY you can awake to a new beginning. Just like repenting of our sins gives us a new beginning in Christ Jesus. Take a deep breath of fresh air and thank Jesus for it and your new start.

'I know your works. Behold, I have set before you an open door, which no one is able to shut. I know that you have but little power, and yet you have kept My Word and have not denied My name.' Revelation 3:8.

That's Memaw...love you

Watch Your Words

Thursday's Thoughts: What Will Your Day End Like?

Complaining opens the door to the devil. In fact, complaining is one of his characteristics.

Israel, while in the desert, chose to complain, over being grateful. They choose to be pitiful instead of power. And look at what happened to them. They died in the desert.
Luke 20:41-44 TLB

But as they (Jesus and His disciples) came closer to Jerusalem and He saw the city (your life) ahead He began to cry and said...eternal peace was within your reach, and you turned it down. He wept saying...and now it's too late. Your enemies will pile up earth (things you put before Christ) against your walls and encircle you, and crush you to the ground, and your children with you. Your enemies will not leave one stone (item) upon another...for you have rejected the opportunity God offered you.

Jesus is coming back soon. What's your life going to end up like?

With every breath I love you...Memaw

Blood Bought

Friday's Fruit: What's In Your Possession?

Possession: a state of having something - an item or property.

In God's Word, possessions are things you own...or things that own you.

You can possess land, houses, cars, stuff, or they can possess you. If your possessions own you, then you are the most miserable. You can even possess yourself. If you are your own possession, then nobody can tell you anything. You are always right, and everyone else is wrong.

If you are possessed by your stuff, you will always be at someone's throat about it. A person possessed by stuff, will have a bitter attitude. Always angry because someone messed with their stuff. But if you look deeply into your stuff through the Word of God, you don't own anything.

You were bought with blood. You can't have life unless you have the blood. Physically or spiritually.

Now compare your stuff with the blood. Which has the most value? You can live without your stuff, but you can't live without the blood.

Luke 12:15 NASB - Then He said to them, “Beware, and be on your guard against every form of greed; for not even when one has an abundance does his life consist of possessions. BOOM.

I love you.... Memaw

Blessed Of The Lord

Saturday's Sayings: So, So Blessed

Has God heard your voice yet today?

Blessed be the LORD, for He has heard my cry for mercy. Psalms 28:6 NIV

Blessed be the LORD, because He has heard the voice of my supplications! KJV

Blessed be Yahweh, because he has heard the voice of my petitions. WEB

God heard David's voice. God wants to hear from the voice He gave you. I can just see Him now, leaning back with His eyes closed, listening to your voice as you talk to Him.

I don't know why we have such a hard time talking to the One who loves us more than anyone else.

Strange, isn't it??

Talk to your LORD. He's waiting.... love Memaw

According To His Will

Sunday's Song: Are You Confident In Him?

And this is the confidence that we have in Him, that whatsoever we ask according to His will, He hears us. And if we know He hears us, we know we have the petition of what we desired of Him.
1JOHN 5:14-15

Have you asked Him anything today?

Did you believe you have what you ask Him?

Amen...love you Memaw

Trusting Or Troubled

Monday's Meditations: Who Do You Trust?

If you are trusting in yourself, then watch out because sometimes, even you can be wrong.

If it's friends, be careful because they don't know what's best for you either.

If it's the government, you are in big trouble.

The ONLY TRUE One to trust is:

Trust in the Lord with all your heart and lean not on your own understanding; in all your ways submit to him,
And he will make your paths straight. Proverbs 3:5-6 NIV

He is NEVER wrong. Even if you don't like His advice, He ALWAYS has the right answer.

Now tell Him with your voice, I trust You Jesus.

...love and joy, Memaw

Take My Yoke

Tuesday's Tips: Where Does Your Heart Lie?

What governs your life?

The word "Govern" means to take authority over something or someone.

What have you given your heart authority over?
Work, kid's, pleasures...things

A mark of a life governed by the Spirit is continually and ever more and more occupied with Christ. Is this true in your case?

That I may know Him. Philippians 3:10 KJV.

At the end of life, it can be said...it pleased God...to reveal His Son in me. Galatians 1:16 KJV.

Jesus was utterly dependent upon God on this earth...are you?

Matthew 11:29 KJV...take My yoke upon you and learn of Me.

Wow. Grace. Peace. Love....Memaw

Wednesday's Word: What Is Your Rooster?

John 13:38 NASB...Jesus answered, "Will you lay down your life for me? Truly, truly, I say to you, the rooster will not crow till you have denied me three times.

A rooster today can be any way of life you choose to live outside the life God designed for you. A job that gives you money by cheating others, a lifestyle that is sinful, disappointments that you want to let go of, offenses where you were hurt, unforgiving others, bitterness, wanting to get even, all these can be roosters.

But I promise you by my own experience that the rooster WILL crow one day. I beg you, kill that rooster today before he has a chance to cause you more shame, guilt, and regret that seems like never ending for years to come.

And then there is Jesus. He will make ALL things new.

It's your choice.

I choose Jesus.

Anointed Words

Thursday's Thoughts: What Is Your Mouth Like?

And He hath made my mouth like a sharp sword; in the shadow of His hand hath He hid me and made me a polished shaft; in His quiver hath He hid me. Isaiah 49:2

One of our most key instruments as representatives of the Gospel is found in our words. It was said of Jesus that His words carried power and authority. Luke 4:32 NIV.

There was obviously something unique anytime Jesus opened His mouth to speak. His words had the power to cast out demons, heal the sick, and calm the storms. We also know that our words carry power. Proverbs 18:21 NIV.

However, even with power in our words, we cannot be fully effective unless we know how to use our words correctly. We need to allow the Lord to polish the things that come from our mouth so we can speak for the Lord with not only power, but tastefully and accurately.

Decree today that your words are divinely anointed and that the sword of the Lord is in your mouth. Powerful...love you Memaw

I AM Knows Me

Friday's Fruit: The Lord Knew Me

The Lord gave me this message this morning: I knew you BEFORE I formed you in your mother's womb. Jeremiah 1:4-5 NLT

The word "knew" in the Greek means - to come to know - recognize - take notice, especially through personal experience, -first hand acquaintance.

God, my Father had a first-hand experience with me before He created me in the womb. And He goes on to say, to be holy and blameless.
Romans 8:29 NLT: For God knew His people in advance, and He chose them to be like His Son, so that His Son would be the FIRSTBORN among many brothers and sisters.

FIRSTBORN I believe, means Jesus was the first to be filled with the Holy Spirit and raised bodily from the dead. So, we will be able to do the same.

God came to earth so we could get to know Him through Jesus. Since God knew us before our creation in the womb, now He wants us to have a first-hand acquaintance with Him. Do you know Him, are you acquainted with Him through Christ? Love and honoring Him...Memaw

Chosen Ones

Saturday's Sayings: How Do You Feel About Yourself And Life?

Do you feel like a reed planted by a riverbank that someone has stepped all over? Bruised? Or were you like the flame that was burning high and aglow, but now it seems like a flicker about to go out? Hurt by someone's words? Maybe you're faint-hearted, because nothing you seem to be doing is going right. Disappointed. Or maybe you are on the verge of despair because you don't feel you measure up to who you think you should be because of what someone has said to you or about you.

Isaiah 42:1-5 NIV...See My Servant, whom I uphold; My chosen One, in whom I delight. I have put My Spirit upon Him; He will reveal justice to the nations of the world. He will be gentle - He will not shout nor quarrel in the streets. He will not break the bruised reed, nor quench the dimly burning flame. He will encourage the faint-hearted, those tempted to despair. He will see full justice given to all who have been wronged. He won't be satisfied until truth and righteousness prevail throughout the earth, nor until distant lands beyond the seas have put their trust in Him.

BOOM

Now take a deep breath and smile. Your Lord just said He will take care of all your circumstances. Love you...Memaw

Sweet Aroma Of Jesus

Sunday's Song: Watch Where You Are Doing.

Oh, the joys of those who do not follow evil men's advice, who do not hang around with sinners, (unbelievers) scoffing at the things of God: But they (we) delight in doing everything God wants them (us) to, and day and night are always meditating on His laws and thinking about ways to follow Him more closely. Psalms 1:1-2 TLB

So your Fruit today is JOY. It's the joy you receive from the Holy Spirit when you follow after Jesus and not the world. Amen

Memaw...she loves you

God Works Through You

Monday's Meditations: What Is Your Life Mission?

Think about it...EVERYTHING you do each day is a mission. Is it making your life and those around you more like Christ's? Is your mission just to acquire acknowledgement, influence, and money for yourself?

1PETER 1:1 TLB ... (starts off saying) From Peter, Jesus Christ's missionary.

To: Christians (everywhere)

Dear friends, God the Father chose you long ago and knew you would become His children. And the Holy Spirit has been at work in your hearts, cleansing you with the blood of Jesus and making you to please Him.

I believe your mission today is to do all you can to let the Holy Spirit do His work. He will do a better job than we can.

I love you...Memaw

Hey..Hey..Hey

That's Southern For Good Morning Yall

Tuesday's Tips: It's Your Choice

1PETER 1:1 -3 TLB....All honor to God, the God and Father of our Lord Jesus Christ; for it is His boundless mercy that has given us the privilege of being born again, so that we are now members of God's own family. Now we live in the hope of eternal life because Christ rose again from the dead.

Now life brings pain, sorrow, trials, heartache, suffering, and disease.

Jesus brings salvation, eternal life, healing, peace, joy, comfort, favor, and forgiveness, and much more.

And you get to choose which one you want.

I love you joyfully...Memaw

Love And Faith

Wednesday's Word: What Are The Two Most Important Things To You?

Well, two of the most important things to God are:

1. LOVE the Lord God with all your heart, mind, and soul. Mark 12:30-31, NIV "And thou shalt love the Lord thy God with all thy heart, and with all thy soul, and with all thy mind, and with all thy strength; this is the first commandment… There is no other commandment greater."

2. Without FAITH it is impossible to please God Hebrews 11:6 NIV" And without faith it is impossible to please God, because anyone who comes to Him must believe that He exists and that He rewards those who earnestly seek Him".

Get it right with God, and EVERYTHING else in your life is right. That doesn't mean you want experience trials; it means you want notice them as trials, just opportunities and tests to strengthen your love and faith in Him.

Amazing

...love you Memaw

For Verily I Say

Thursday's Thoughts: Do You Believe What You Say?

Have faith in God.

For verily I say unto you, that whosoever shall say unto this mountain, be thou removed and be thou cast into the sea; and shall not doubt in his heart but shall believe that those things which he said shall come to pass; he shall have whatsoever he said. Mark 11:22-24 KJV

Everything you say and believe is what you get.

That means you either say and believe what Jesus said or you say and believe what Satan says.

I believe Jesus...I love you...Memaw

Friday's Fruit: What Message Do You Have That I Need To Hear?

Is your message about what you or your children have accomplished?

Is your message what a horrible life you have?
Is your message belittling others?
Is your message always about you?

Your message is what you say, what you believe, and how you live, before the world.

John 17:20 TLB.... Jesus said, I pray not only for these, (His 11 disciples) but also for those (believers) who believe in Me through their message.

What message, do the people you talk to hear?
Can they believe in Jesus because of your message?

Note: sanctified means living, looking, and acting differently than the world. Set apart from the way the world lives. Set apart to live for

Christ. Are you?

I love you...and that's my message...Memaw

Power In His Name

Saturday's Sayings: What Do You Have?

You HAVE what you say. If you say you HAVE a headache...guess what? You have it. If you say you HAVE no time...again, you don't have time. If you say you HAVE been run over by a reindeer. Boom, you have. Repeat...you HAVE what you say.

But Jesus says, Say what you HAVE. Say you are healed in Jesus' name. Say you are forgiven. Say you are sanctified. Say you are blessed. Say you have abundance. All in Jesus' name. Because you surely can't have what you say without using the power that comes from His name.

But there is a condition to using His name. It's believing His name has power. If you don't believe He will do what He says He will do, then what you say is just a pile of words that have no use in them. I will prove what I tell you is true from God's Word.

And Peter, remembering, said to Him, "Rabbi, look! The fig tree which You cursed has withered away." Then Jesus answered and said to them, "Have faith in God. For assuredly, I say to you, whoever says" to this mountain, 'Be removed and be cast into the sea,' and does not doubt in him heart, but believes that those things he says will be done, he will have whatever he says." Mark 11:23-24. KJV

Your words speak volumes.

Are your words helping or hurting yourself and others?

If you know Jesus' Word and speak it and believe it to be true, it's yours.

So, I speak I love you with His life. Memaw

NOTE: the mountain is ANY problem, situation, or circumstance. Jesus said what He will do about it. If you are sick, He will heal you, tired He will strengthen you, sinned He will forgive you.

What's your problem? Jesus has a fix.

Setting Boundaries

Sunday's Song: Do You Have Boundaries?

God does. God set boundaries for land, ocean and sea perimeters, trees, animals, plants and people perimeters.

You can find what His boundaries are in His Word.

God spoke to me this morning and said; what are your boundaries?

Are your boundaries godly? Or, are they so strict that they harm instead of help?

Are your boundaries so loose that you allow anyone to dictate how you live?

If you don't set boundaries for living the way you know God wants you to live, then others will impose their boundaries on you.

When you live under God's boundaries, you are living a most happy life. If you live under other people's boundaries, you will live the most miserable life.

If you get mad and angry when someone tells you their boundaries, that they know God has set for them, then you have trouble with love.

If you have no boundaries set for yourself, then others will be allowed to bring the way they want you to live into your life, even if its sin.

As I said, God spoke. Now I need to listen.

Ephesians 5:7-9 ESV says, so have nothing to do with them. In the past, you were full of darkness, but now you are full of light in the Lord. So, live like children who belong to the light. Light brings every kind of goodness, right living, and truth.

2Corithians 6:16 ESV says, do not be unequally yoked with unbelievers. For what partnership has righteousness with lawlessness? Or what fellowship has light with darkness?

1Corithians 5:11 ESV says, but I am writing to you not to associate with anyone who bears the name of brother if he is guilty of sexual immorality or greed, or is an idolater, reviler, drunkard, or swindler – not even to eat with such a one.

Psalm 1:1 ESV says, blessed is the man who walks not in the counsel of the wicked, nor stands in the way of sinners, nor sits in the seat of scoffers.

1Corintians 15:33 ESV says, do not be deceived: “Bad company ruins good morals.”

Blessings and favor…. Memaw

Resurrected Life

Monday's Meditations: Remembering Jesus

This morning after I woke from sleep Jesus asked me; do you know what it's like to lose it all? Where, you literally only have your clothes? Job gone, family left, friends no longer have anything to do with you. No roof over your head. Truly lost everything. And the ONLY thing you have is Him. I had to say, no Lord, I don't know what it's like. Sometimes I thought I was close but never experienced losing everything.

Jesus said until you lose it all you will never completely have Me, because when you don't think I am your every source you will rely on what you have.

I know Jesus has provided for me and protected me my entire life. But until I have nothing but Him, I don't have anything.

Sunday is Resurrection Day. Can't you for a moment lose everything and remember what He did? It's called Communion. The Lord's Supper. Prepare your heart to remember His blood and body that He gave up heaven for a while for you.

Remember Him...I love you Memaw

By His Standards And Measurements

Tuesday’s Tips: What Are Your Standards?

A standard is: something you establish as a rule. Either by someone's authority, custom or example. Standards are a way of measuring or valuing how we live or how we decide things.

Have you set up standards on how you live? Are your standards yours or God's? By whose standards do you measure yourself and others?

Your standards might have the tendency to criticize, put down, judge or slander others because they don't measure up to your standards.

Your standards can cause bitterness towards others, jealousy, envy, or condemnation.

But if you set your standards on God's standards, the way He values and measures people and their situations, your life will be joyful, grateful, and thankful.

Thus, saith the Lord GOD, Behold, I will lift up mine hand to the Gentiles, and set up my standard to the people: and they shall bring thy sons in their arms, and thy daughters shall be carried upon their shoulders. Isaiah 49:22 KJV

We do not dare to classify or compare ourselves with those who commend themselves. When they measure themselves by themselves and compare themselves with themselves, they show their ignorance.

2CORITHIANS 10:12 NIV

Love you with the measure of Christ...Memaw

Magnifying Him

Wednesday's Word: Magnify God, Not Yourself Or Your Problem

Magnify is to make something bigger than it truly is.

To Magnify yourself or your situation is manufacturing your own misery. Or as grandma used to say "you're making a mountain out of a mole hill."

To Magnify God is to extol, glorify, praise, bless, or worship Him.

Oh, Magnify the Lord with me, and let us exalt His name together. Psalms 35:26 KJV

The more you Magnify God the bigger He gets in your life and your problem gets smaller.

I chose today to Magnify God.

I love you Memaw

God's Promises Kept

Thursday's Thoughts: Do You Keep Your Word?

God told Abraham at 90 years old that he would have a son, and not just a son, but an impossible act of conceiving a human by the time he was 100 years old. And God kept His promise.

I want you to hear this, children. IF GOD PROMISES TO DO SOMETHING HE ALWAYS, ALWAYS, ALWAYS CARRIES IT OUT, unless YOU doubt, HE will.

If God says, He will forgive your sins, every one of them, past, present and future, with the one-time death AND resurrection of His Son Jesus AND you believe that God WILL KEEP HIS PROMISE, it's a done deal.

But that's not the only promise God made you. He wrote down His promises, He made a contract with you and signed that contract with the blood of His Son Jesus.

ALL God's promises are yours if you believe them enough to thank Him for them before you receive them.

Do you truly thank Jesus for what He did for you? If you truly believe all His promises are for you, then you will sense your heart crying with gratitude.

For God so loved you that He gave His Son, for and to you. And I give my heart to Him, so I can have Him and every promise He made me.

If you are saved by Jesus' blood, and promised Him your heart and life, are you keeping your promise to Him?

I love you, Memaw

The Holy Spirit's Work

Friday's Fruit: Examine Your Heart

Your heart reveals who you are.

Galatians 5:22-23 NIV But the fruit of the Spirit is love, joy, peace, forbearance, kindness, goodness, faithfulness, gentleness, and self-control. Against such things there is no law.

Did you notice these characteristics are produced in you by the Holy Spirit?

Something else was interesting. The first fruit is love.

Without love, it is very hard to possess the other fruits. In fact, I don't believe the Holy Spirit can work the other fruits in us unless we truly possess love.

Genuine love gives the Holy Spirit the ability to work out the other fruits He wants to produce in us. Without love, you have no joy, peace, forbearance, patience, kindness, goodness, faithfulness, gentleness, or self-control. All that is left is confusion, sadness, vengeance, turmoil, guilt, shame, anger, and pain.

I chose love. Even when those around me are not loveable. Because I have no idea what they are dealing with and I want others to love me when I don't display loveable actions.

Favor...I love you Memaw

Love One Another

Saturday's Sayings: How Do You Love?

A new commandment I give unto you, that ye love one another; as I have loved you, that ye also love one another. John 13:34 NIV

Do you? Do you love others as Jesus loves you? Do you keep His commandment?

I love you as He loves you.... Memaw

Tell The Next Generation

Sunday's Song: Who Ys your Guide?

How about Proverbs?

Proverbs 27:19 NLT...As a face is reflected in water, so the heart reflects the real person.

V10...Never abandon a friend, either yours or your father's. When disaster strikes, you won't have to ask your brother for assistance.

V12...A prudent person foresees danger and takes precautions. The simpleton goes blindly on and suffers the consequences.

V18... As workers who tend a fig tree are allowed to eat the fruit, so workers who protect their employer's interest will be rewarded.

I love you.... Memaw

Psalm 78:4 NIV

We will not hide these truths from our children but will tell the next generation about the glorious deeds of the Lord, we will tell of His power and mighty miracles He did.

It Takes Only One Step

Monday's Meditations: Do You Live In Christ?

She......laid Him in a manger, because there was no room for them in the inn. Luke 2:7 KJV

Foxes have holes and birds of the air have nests, but the Son of Man has nowhere to lay His head. Matthew 8:20 NIV

Is this true of your life?

Have you given Jesus a place to live with you?

People love Jesus, they want Him, yet they dare not have Him in their homes. If Jesus came to our homes, the words He spoke would so convict us that we couldn't stand in His presence. We believe He is holy, lovely and beautiful, yet we don't want Him to be in our homes.

Because He didn't have a place to lay His head, He spent the night on the Mt of Olives.

Does Jesus have a place to lay His head in your home?
People don't want Jesus in their homes because of the changes they would have to make in their lives. Will you invite Him in your home? Are you willing to change your life for Him to have a place to lay His

head?

It is only one step to Jesus.

I love you...Memaw

Building Your Faith

Tuesday's Tips: How Do You Go About Your Day And Life?

Then Jesus was led by the Spirit into the wilderness to be tempted there by the devil. Matthew 4:1 NIV

As Jesus was led each day of His life here on earth by the Holy Spirit, we who are His should do the same.

Jesus was able to conquer every temptation of the devil because He committed Himself to being led by the Holy Spirit. So can we.

Do you know why sometimes we go through bad situations? It's because God is trying to build your faith in Jesus, to help you in relying on the Holy Spirit and training you in rebuking the devil so he will flee from you.

God loves you. He is training you like you are training your children, to become stronger children of His.

So don't fret the devilish small stuff, rely on Christ, He's got you covered.

I chose to be Spirit led today...Memaw

Fruit Of A Good Tree

Wednesday's Word: What Kind Of Fruit Are You Bearing?

Luke 6:43-45 NLT...Jesus says.... A good tree (person) cannot produce bad fruit. A bad tree (person) cannot produce good fruit. Figs are never gathered from thornbushes. Grapes are not picked from bramble bushes. A good person produces good things from the treasury of a good heart. An evil person produces evil things from the treasury of an evil heart. What you say flows from what is in your heart.

Thank you, Jesus.

I love you, Jesus....Memaw

Applying Fruit

Thursday's Thoughts: How Do You Get Your Fruit?

This is how I found where my Fruit from God comes from.

If I pray for more love, the Holy Spirit will put me around unlovable people so I can love like Jesus.

When I ask for peace, I will be given unsettling circumstances so I can learn to receive the peace Jesus left me.

As I ask for faith, things in my life may become wobbly just so the faith I have will grow.

If I ask for joy, I will hear concerning news so I will learn to sense the presence of God.

Sounds like God is teaching us that we have been given Him through Christ and all these characteristics of His are ours and all we have to do is use them as needed.

So, when you find yourself up against trying circumstances God your Father is watching you apply His gifts in your life.

So good...love you Memaw.

He Has Triumphed

Friday's Fruit: What Does Your Life SMELL Like?

Does your life smell so much like something dead, that no one wants to hear what you have to say?

God says...But thanks be to God! For through what Christ has done, He has triumphed over us so that now wherever we go, He uses us to tell others about the Lord and to spread the Gospel like a sweet perfume. As far as God is concerned, there is a sweet, wholesome fragrance in our lives. It is the fragrance of Christ within us, an aroma to both the saved and the unsaved all around us. To those who are not being saved, we seem a fearful smell of death and doom, while to those who know Christ, we are a life-giving perfume. But who is adequate for such a task as this? Only those who, like ourselves, are men of integrity, sent by God, speaking with Christ's power, with God's eye upon us. We are not like those hucksters - and there are many of them - whose idea in getting out of the Gospel is to make a good living out of it. 2CORITHIANS 2:14-17 TLB

Take a deep breath in God's Word and smell what your life should be like

...love you so much...Memaw

Mediate Day And Night

Saturday’s Sayings: What Does It Mean To Meditate?

It’s to think deeply or focus your mind on something.

God instructs us to meditate. He says in Psalms 1:2 NLT...they delight in the law of the LORD, meditating on it day and night. And in Joshua 1:8 NIV…. Keep this book of the law on your lips; meditate on it day and night, so that you may be careful to do everything written in it. Then you will be prosperous and successful.

So, let's meditate on this today. Your heavenly Father will forgive you if you forgive those who sin against you; but if you refuse to forgive them, God will not forgive you. Matthew 6:14-15 NIV

Focus on this: Those who know they are forgiven.... forgive.

And... if you wanted what God had for you, your heart would yearn to go get it.

Thinking about you with love...Memaw

When Your Fruit Is Squeezed

Sunday's Song: What Do You Have.... Inside?

When you are about to move in a certain direction remember...it's only one step to Jesus.

Think about the hurts you have experienced from a friend or family member? Now think about the beating Jesus took. Which one experienced the worse hurt? Jesus' hurt prepared Him for our eternal life. Could your trials be getting you ready for your presentation before the Lord.

What's inside will come out as Proverbs 27:19 NIV says: as water reflects the face, so a man's heart reveals the man.

Rejoicing in Christ for you...I love you ...Memaw

Grace From God

Monday's Meditations: What Does God Want For You?

Last night, the storm was raging outside our home. But inside was peace and calm. And it is what God wants for His children.

Paul, a slave of Christ, as he calls himself in the book of Philippians in the TLB tells us some of the things God wants for us.

Paul says in chapter 1, verse 2. May God bless you all. I pray that God our Father AND the Lord Jesus Christ give you His fullest blessing. (Not just any blessings, but so much of His blessings that they flow out of you) Paul goes on to ask God to give you peace in your hearts and lives. Then he says his prayers for you are full of praise to God. Paul is praying for us and not himself.

What are your prayers about? You or others?

In verse 7 he shares with the Philippians how they have a special place in his heart and it was because they defended the truth and told others about Christ. And that's what God wants from you, to tell others about His Son.

Out of this chapter I also saw that my Father wants to bless me, give me His peace, to praise Him, receive His grace and love, and to know the difference between right and wrong. Just to name a few.

He is a good Father and He wants to give you Jesus and all His blessings come with Him.

I bless you and love you in Jesus' name...Memaw

Treasured And Valued

Tuesday's Tips: What Do You Value?

What you think about and talk about is what you value the most.

What you talk about most could be your job, children, sports, cars, or yourself.

There is nothing you don't know about the subject you value and love.

What about God? Does He have any value to you?

The things you value the most are the things you put your money, time, energy, and study into. The things you value most are the things you put your urgency into.

If you have something so valuable to you that you would swim a raging river for, then that valuable thing has become your god. Kid's, I have an urgency in my spirit so strong that it feels as if I don't tell you everything God is sharing with me, I will burst. And you would be to if you value God and Jesus and His Word. This is what God said to me.

We will not hide these truths from our children, we will tell the next generation about the glorious deeds of the Lord, about His power and His mighty wonders. For He issued His laws to Jacob, He gave His instruction to Israel. He COMMANDED our ancestors to teach them to their children, so the next generation might know them - (listen children) even the children not yet born - and they in turn will teach their own children.

Psalms 78:4-6 NIV.

Put your value on God and His Word, then your children will know how to value Him.

I value and love Jesus and you... Just preaching Memaw

Wisdom Brings Life

Wednesday's Word: Where Does Your Wisdom Come From?

Proverbs is a "collection of collections" that teaches values, moral behavior, and the meaning of human life, that "the fear of God (meaning submission to the will of God) is the beginning of wisdom". Wisdom is praised for her role in creation; God acquired her before all else, and through her, he gave order to chaos; and seeking wisdom is the essence of life.

A few things wisdom teaches:

1. Proverbs 11:1 TLB ...the Lord hates cheating and delights in dishonesty
2. Proud men end in shame, but the meek become wise.
3. A good man is guided by his honesty; the evil man is destroyed by his dishonesty.
4. Your riches won't help you on judgment day; only your righteousness counts then.

Choose wisdom, she will always be your friend, never make you do something wrong and will keep you out of trouble.

I love you...Memaw

All For His Glory

Thursday's Thoughts: What You Can Do Today:

Whatever you do, do ALL for the glory of God.
1Corinthian 10:31 NIV

Hold fast to the LORD your God. Joshua 23:8

As new babies, desire the pure milk of the Word, that you may grow thereby. 1PETER 2:2 NKJV

Have faith in God. Mark 11:22 NIV

And last, but not all....

Do ALL things without complaining and disputing, that you may become blameless and harmless, children of God without fault in the midst of a crooked and perverse generation, among whom you shine as lights in the world. Philippians 2:14-15

Say amen to Jesus...I love you, Memaw

Friday's Fruit: Is God Pointing His Finger At You?

All night, I have had a grieving spirit within me. I believe someone in our family should be warned. I believe someone needs to be warned to watch out you are about to be burned. Satan is trying to entrap you. He is a liar. ANYTHING contrary to God's Word is a ball face satanic lie.

Have I told you today that I love every one of you? Have I told you I need each of you? To the ones who were born into my life and to the ones that became mine because you said "I DO" I love you.

The devil knows your habits, your behavior, and he knows how to trap you. He knows by the way you have responded before that you were unhappy, disappointed, angry, or not nice to others. He knows how to trap us by our fleshy desires.

As I opened my Bible this morning, this is where it landed.

Hosea 4: TLB God says; Hear the Word of the Lord, O people. The Lord has filed a lawsuit (a charge) against you. There is NO kindness, NO knowledge of God in your land (heart). You swear and lie and steal (take another person's trust in you from them) and commit adultery. There is violence everywhere, one murder after another. V3 your land (life) is not producing, it is filled with sadness. V4. Do NOT point your finger at someone else and put the blame on him. Look, I (God) am pointing My finger at you. God goes on to say you will fall in broad daylight and night. You are destroying people. Please read the rest of this chapter. I didn't want to do this, but God has said tell them. I am just being obedient to my Lord.

God also told me that He has placed my family in a womb and He doesn't want ANY ONE ABORTED., by divorce.

Love and grace...Memaw

God's Heart Of Mercy

Saturday's Sayings: What Is Abortion?

This is what I learned from God about abortion. And what He said broke my heart. God said every one of us has committed an abortion at some point in our life.

So, I looked up the definition of abortion. 1. The "deliberate" termination of a human being. 2. The "expulsion" of a fetus from the womb. 3. An "undertaking" of doing away with something in regard to an unpleasant situation.

I ask my Lord, how had I carried out an abortion. His answer, when you disobey My Word. When you tell a lie to get what you want. When you fail to uphold your word. When you blame others for your mess. When you hurt another person for the sake of your own life, when you are selfish, self-centered, and to you, everyone else is wrong. When you do these things deliberately to expel people who, love and trust us, out of our life. They don't have any value, they are not worth saving, so you throw them out like garbage. If they interfere with your wants, you discard them from your life. You break their lives apart to get your way. And last He said, living your life apart from Me you have aborted Me also. My heart is broken. I never thought of myself as an abortionist. God does not mince His Word. But He never stops loving or abort us when we sin. He forgives. From His heart...I love you, Memaw

Morning Loving Children.

Sunday's Song: Fruits Of The Flesh

Lately, I have shared the Fruits of the Spirit with you from Galatians 5:22-23.

Today God has turned me to teach you about the fruit of the flesh from Galatians 5:13-21 NIV. Which says: You, my brothers and sisters, were called to be free. But do not use your freedom to indulge the flesh, rather, serve one another humbly in love. For the entire law is fulfilled in keeping this one command: "Love your neighbor as yourself." If you bite and devour each other, watch out or you will be destroyed by each other. So, I say, walk by the Spirit, and you will not gratify the desires of the flesh. For the flesh desires what is contrary to the Spirit, and the Spirit what is contrary to the flesh. They are in conflict with each other, so that you are not to do whatever you want. But if you are led by the Spirit, you are not under the law. The acts of the flesh are obvious: (you can see them clearly) sexual immorality, impurity and debauchery; idolatry and witchcraft; hatred, discord, jealousy, fits of rage, selfish ambition, dissensions, factions and envy; drunkenness, orgies, and the like. I warn you, as I did before, that those who live like this will not inherit the kingdom of God.

After reading this scripture it seemed odd to me that God only list 9 characteristics of the Fruit of the Spirit, but He list 17 fruit characteristics of the flesh.

This is what I discovered.

#1. Sexual immorality: adultery, unfaithfulness of a husband or wife, lust, a strong desire for a person not your spouse.

Is your Fruit Spirit or flesh?

Looking in the Bible to find justification for your sin can only be found in Jesus.

DEEPLY loving you...Memaw

Morning Delight Of Jesus

Monday's Meditations: Who Do You Look Like, Flesh Or Spirit?

Fleshy Fruit 1: Sexual immorality. Adultery, unfaithfulness of a husband or wife, lust, a strong desire for a person not your spouse.

Jesus tells us in Matthew 5:27-30 NIV. You have heard that it was said, you shall not commit adultery.' But I say to you that everyone who looks at a woman with lustful intent has already committed adultery with her in his heart.

You don't even have to carry out the sin in the physical, just desire to do it, and you have committed it.

I wonder how many times a day, for the rest of her life, did Satan remind Eve that she ate the fruit of disobedience?

The difference is, no matter the sin, Jesus forgives upon repentance, but Satan never lets you forget it.

Sounds like a Spirit life is a very good thing compared to a flesh life. I am His...with love for you Memaw

Living By His Power

Tuesday's Tips: What Are You Inclined To Do Today?

Inclined means: to turn away from or lean into doing something. Example: are you turning away from God for your own desires or are you leaning on Him and His Word for direction.

Galatians 5: 19 -TLB puts it this way, but when you follow your own "inclinations" your lives will produce these results: impure thoughts, eagerness for lustful pleasure, idolatry, spiritism, (that is encouraging the activity of demons) hatred and fighting, jealousy, constant effort to get the best for yourself, complaints and criticisms, the feeling that everyone else is wrong except those in your own little group - and there will be wrong doctrine, envy, murder, drunkenness, wild parties and ALL sorts of other things.

Again, what are you inclined to do today?

If you follow after God, you won't be inclined to live the life like the ones listed above.

Verse 25 - If we are living by the POWER of the Holy Spirit, let us FOLLOW His leading in every part of our lives.

I love you.... Memaw

Look Inside

Wednesday's Word: What's Inside Your Heart?

The last few days, I have been teaching you about the fruit of the flesh.

Galatians 5:13 NLT says ... you have been called to live in freedom...but don't use your freedom to satisfy your sinful nature.... use your freedom to SERVE one another in love.

So, as papa and I read God's Word today in our devotion time together, I believe Jesus was referring to our freedom. Your freedom comes from what is inside you. Your heart.

Mark 7:20-23 NLT...it is what comes from inside, that defiles you. For from within, out of a person's heart, comes evil thoughts, sexual immorality, theft, murder, adultery, greed, wickedness, deceit, lustful desires, envy, slander, pride, and foolishness. ALL these vile things come from within; they are what defile you.

So don't go blaming someone else for the problems you made that came from your heart. Look inside.

Feeding the children in Jesus' name with love...Memaw

Breath Taking

Thursday's Thoughts: Who Do You Follow?

You are beautiful children, but you're also breathing His air.

Yesterday God's Word said in Galatians 5:13 NIV that we have been given freedom to do what is right. To love and serve each other. Verse 15 says, but instead of showing love to others you criticize and claw at each other. Verse 16...God said, I advise you to obey only the Holy Spirit's instructions. He will tell you where to go and what to do. Then you won't always be doing the wrong things your evil nature wants to do. For we (you and me) love to do evil things that are just the opposite from the things that the Holy Spirit tells us to do.

Doing evil things is our nature, which is the nature of Satan. That's why we are to fight and fight and fight the good fight. Fighting to do right is hard...in the natural. But it's easy in the Spirit. Again, who do you follow? The Father that gives you the very air you breathe, or the father of lies.

By your actions and words, who are you teaching your children to follow?

Friday's Fruit: What Do You Not Have, That You Want?

Jesus said to me...I did not take a lesser stripe for telling a lie, being angry with my spouse, or jealousy than I did for murder or adultery. The stripes I took were all equally painful for ALL your sins. The stripes were because of your sins, not mine.

Question: What is it that you don't have that is making you so unhappy?

In Jesus, there is no unfulfilled wants. When you don't feel loved, you are unfulfilled. If you FULLY love Jesus, you can't be unfulfilled.

Question: Do you love being miserable every day? Love Jesus, and your miserable life goes away.

If you're miserable with what you have now, then give it all up, or you will find more misery. God does not give you a miserable life. We make our lives miserable by our choices.

Philippians 4:4-8 NIV...Rejoice in the Lord always: and again, I say, Rejoice. Let your moderation be known unto all men. The Lord is at hand. Be careful for nothing; but in everything by prayer and supplication, with thanksgiving, let your requests be made known unto God. And the peace of God, which passeth all understanding, shall keep your hearts and minds through Christ Jesus. Finally, brethren, whatsoever things are true, whatsoever things are honest, whatsoever things are just, whatsoever things are pure, whatsoever things are lovely, whatsoever things are of good report; if there be any virtue, and if there be any praise, think on these things.

Choosing to rejoice in all things...love you Memaw

Looking Through????

Saturday's Sayings: What Do You See?

What you are seeing is what you're looking at, or what you are using to look through. If you're looking at how miserable you are, you are looking through your eyes. If you're looking at how beautiful EVERYTHING around you is, even your problems, then you are looking through your heart. If you and your spouse are not getting through to each other, try looking through your heart at them and not your eyes. Remember each of you said, "I do". What happened? What did you think "I do" meant? Were you looking at love, security, peace, joy, comfort, enjoyment or for money, influence, a way out, or prestige?

Pastor Chris asks a couple seeking divorce did they say they married for better or worse. They both said yes. Then he asked them, what did they think "worse" was supposed to look like. What does worse look like to you? It looks like whatever eyes you're using.

I pray that the eyes of your heart may be enlightened in order that you may know the hope to which He has called you, the riches of His glorious inheritance in His holy people. Ephesians 1:8

Loving you with the eyes of my heart...Memaw

Sunday's Song: What Cha Thinking?

Yesterday morning as I was brushing my teeth, I asked Jesus what love was supposed to look like, His answer.... forgiveness.

Joyce Myers said there were 5,467 promises God had written in the Bible. Ever how many of them you want, God will give by faith.

It seems to me that we, this family, is so troubled by our flesh's wants, that we don't have any desire for Jesus.

Our wants have robbed us of peace, contentment, joy, comfort, delight, and faith.

Because we can't have our way, we become disappointed in others.

Memaw is going to get tuff right now. Have you been beaten until blood oozed from your body; have you been locked in dark places that had no light for long periods of time? Have you been ridiculed publicly for who you were, been mocked and criticized for telling the truth, shamed for your appearance, sexually assaulted many times? And I could list more, but if your answer is no, I haven't experienced any of those things, then your little disappointments for not getting your way doesn't hold water. So, if I were in your shoes, I think I would reconsider that my life is amazing and more blessed than I could have dreamed. I am the MOST loved child God has, and I know this because He was the One that brought me through all the above.

You are loved, because you are forgiven. I am who I am because of Him.

Grateful....Memaw

I have shown you in every way, by laboring like this, that you must support the weak. And remember the words of the Lord Jesus, that He said, 'It is more blessed to give than to receive. Acts 20:35 NKJV

Rescued

Monday's Meditations: What Do You Believe About God?

I believe I live under the shadow of God's Almightiness and sheltered by Him because He is the God of ALL gods. He alone is my refuge, my place of safety. He is my God and I am trusting Him. He rescues me from every trap set to harm me. And He protects me from the fatal plagues. He will shield and protect me with His wings. His faithful promises are my armor. I don't need to fear the darkness, the danger of day, the dread of plagues or disaster. Though thousands and ten thousand are dying around me, the evil will not touch me. I will see how the wicked are punished but I will not share any of it, for Jehovah is my refuge! I choose the God above all gods to shelter me. How can evil overtake me or plague come near? Because my God orders His angels to protect me wherever I go. They will steady me with their hands and keep me from stumbling as I go through life. For my Lord says of me: "because Memaw loves me, I will rescue her. I will make her great because she trusts in my name.

And when she calls on me, I will answer. I, her Lord, will be with her IN trouble (didn't say I would not have trouble) and rescue her AND honor her. I will satisfy her with long life and give her MY salvation. Psalms 91. This I believe of my Lord...and with love I believe in you...Memaw

Friend's, Godly Or Godless

Tuesday's Tips: Who Is Your Friend?

And Jesus said unto him, Friend, wherefore art thou come? Then came they, and laid hands-on Jesus, and took Him. Matthew 26:50 KJV

After years of reading Gods Word, I still have no idea what Jesus, in His humanity was going through, in the garden the night He was betrayed. When Judas betrayed Jesus, He did not call him a traitor. He did not call him a back stabber. He called him friend. I don't think Jesus was just trying to be nice either. Jesus always called things the way He saw them. He was straight forward even with the Pharisees calling them white washed sepulchers and brood of vipers. Jesus knew His war was not with flesh and blood, but against Satan.

Matthew 25: 50 KJV says look past the faults of those around us and only see friends as Christ did on the night He was betrayed. The next verse 51 reads, "And, behold, one of them which was with Jesus stretched out [his] hand, and drew his sword, and struck a servant of the high priests, and smote off his ear."

In Peter's zeal to do right, he cuts off the ear of a soldier arresting Jesus. We read how Jesus heals the ear and rebukes Peter, who meant well, but just went too far.

Have I ever spoken a word in the defense of truth that hurt someone needlessly? I am afraid I have. I have asked Jesus to do for me what He did for Peter and heal the person that I needlessly wounded.

Even in Gethsemane Jesus never stopped healing. He is a healing Jesus!

Friends, are yours godly or godless. A godly friend will talk to you about Jesus; a godless friend will talk about sinful desires. A godly friend will encourage and build you up in your walk with Jesus, a godless friend will bring you to godless places and godless conversations.

Pastor Chris says show me your friends and I will show you your future.

Friends...what does your friends look like? Godly or godless?

A godly friend will take a beating for you; a godless friend will watch you get beat up.

I love you, friends. Memaw

Throw Out Your Net

Wednesday's Word: What Would Happen If You Obeyed Jesus?

Luke 5:4-5 NIV...And when He had finished speaking, He said to Simon, "Put out into the deep and let down your nets for a catch." And Simon answered, "Master, we toiled all night and took nothing! But at Your word I will let down the nets." And when they had done this, they enclosed a large number of fish, and their nets were breaking.

This scripture is not just a story about Peter's fishing abilities. What I see is Jesus asking Peter to go further with Him. Don't stay in the same place doing the same thing over and over for Jesus than you did yesterday. Next, Peter, being like most of us, starts making excuses that he has tried going out for the Gospel, but he didn't get any results. But because Christ has asked him to, he will do it again, regardless of the outcome.

Ministry is for Jesus, not our ego. I am going to step out today and challenge every one of you to tell three people that you gave your life to Christ. The first time will feel a little awkward, but the next two times will give you a sense of power and confidence in Jesus that you didn't know existed in you. And last, look at what happens. It may not have changed them, but it will change you. Come on, throw out your net (faith) and see what you catch.

Throwing my net (faith) in Christ...with love Memaw

Thursday's Thoughts: What Is Your Response?

It is the purpose of God for you to rise to the place of sonship. Don't miss the purpose God has for you. Realize that God wants to make you the firstfruits and separate you unto Himself. God will restore those He called, and justify those He called, and those justified, God will also glorify. Romans 8:30

But there must be a response from you to this call. It does not matter who is against us...If God is for us, who can be against us. If there are millions against you, God has a purposed it and will bring you right through to glory. It is with the heart that one believes unto righteousness. Romans 10:10

Do you need to be healed of a critical spirit. Scripture warns: who shall bring a charge against God's elect? It's bad business to harm God's anointed. 1Chron.16:22. The devil is the accuser of the brethren. Rev.12:10. Do not let the devil cripple and bind you. There is a blessed place in the Holy Spirit. Instead of condemning you, Christ is interceding for you. Because God has called and chosen you, He wants you to know that you have power with Him.

Love you...Memaw

The Three Are One

Friday's Fruit: Which ONE Are You?

This morning, around 4ish I listened as God began teaching me about ONE. The ONE began with one God, one Lord, one Holy Spirit. But the three are ONE. Ephesians 4:5-6.

Then He reminded me there is ONE male and ONE female. Genesis 5:2. The male and female marry and the two become ONE. Mark10:8.

When you believe on the Lord Jesus Christ as your Lord, you become ONE with Christ. 1CORITHIANS 12:12-13.

Then God said when ONE sins, he hurts himself. When ONE in a marriage sins, he hurts the marriage. When ONE in a family sin, he hurts the entire family. When ONE in a church sin, it hurts the entire church. (Or it should) The point God made to me was I am not alone in this world He created me in. Whatever I choose to do affects everyone that is ONE with me. Good or bad. The sins I do are not just my sin, because it causes others to sin. So, in a nutshell my choices will be how those in my ONE life will choose to live. Even my attitude will affect others in life. As our body has many parts, our life affects many people.

With ONE love...I love you...Memaw

Guided By The Holy Spirit

Saturday's Sayings: Producing Good Fruit

What kind of fruit are you producing? Is it ripe for harvest or withered up and soured on your vine?

Love, joy, peace, patience, kindness, goodness, faithfulness, gentleness, and self-control are the fruit that God develops in you, because of who He is and who He wants you to be.

Or, is your fruit impure thoughts, eagerness for lustful pleasure, idolatry, spiritism, (encouraging the activity of demons) hatred and fighting, jealousy and anger (jealousy is a form of anger, look at your motive for being angry) constant effort to get the best for yourself, complaining and criticism, feel that everyone else is wrong except you and your group, believing wrong doctrine, envy, murder drunkenness, wild parties and all OTHER sorts of things. (In other words, this is not all the evil people do)

Galatians 5:18 ...when you are guided by the Holy Spirit you need no longer force yourself to obey Jewish (worldly) laws.

Guess what, the Holy Spirit is the one who has the Fruit. Follow Him.

Now go out today and give someone your fruit from God.

..love you Memaw

A Father's Letter

Sunday's Song: Who's Hero, Are You?

A concerned father wrote this letter to the sports coach at his son's school.

"Dear Coach, I just read your letter to our son telling us of your expectations for your athletes. Johnny's mother and I couldn't agree more. We've long recognized the value derived from high school sports. Judging from your record, you must teach the game very well. But there is another phase of coaching that's even more important. Let me explain. We're giving you our most prized possession. During the next four years our son will make you one of our prime household conversations. He'll tell us how you could've made the team for the Green Bay Packers if only you hadn't hurt your knee back in '85. He'll tell us about your emotional halftime talk when you came from behind and beat a rival team. We'll hear about how you can still pass or kick the ball. And while we're hearing all this, our son's eyes will shine. You see, coach, he'll idolize you. We don't have heroes anymore. Many professionals would sell their souls for a buck. Some college athletes made the news this year in a very negative manner. We know all athletes don't shoplift and do drugs, but that's what we hear about. So, you're our son's hero, and we're relying on you. His muscles are nearly developed, but his mind is still fragile and impressionable. Your responsibilities are great. Impress him, Coach. Pour it on! The world's full of gangs, drugs, and violence because a kid picked the wrong hero. You can help change all that - if only for one child.

Think about it.

I love you guys...Memaw

God This Way

Monday's Meditations: Cheer Up, Says The Holy One.

O My people...you shall weep no more, for God will be gracious to you at the sound of your cry. He will answer you. Though He gives you the bread of adversity, yet He will be with you and teach you - with your own eyes you will see your Teacher. And if you leave God's path and go astray, you will hear a Voice behind you say, "No, this is the way, walk here. Isaiah 30:19-21 TLB

Listen to the Voice of your Father. He keeps His promises.

I will free you from your oppression. I will rescue you from the slavery of the world. I will redeem you with a powerful arm and great acts of judgment. I will claim you as my own people, and I will be your God.

Exodus 6:6-7 NIV

Believe every Word He says...love Memaw

Looking To Jesus

Tuesday's Tips: No Other

...there is NO other place to have your eyes but on Jesus.

NO other life will please you.

No other love will satisfy you.

No other peace will comfort you.

No other person will be faithful to the end.

Jesus is looking at you. And He can't help you, unless you look at Him. Wherever you are in life, turn to Jesus.

Blessings...Memaw

Wednesday's Word: What Makes You Happy?

Psalms 119:1—3 TLB...says it all.

Happy are ALL who perfectly follow the laws of God. Happy are ALL who search for God, and always do His will, rejecting comprise with evil, and walking only in His paths.

With God, you are NEVER confused, disappointed, frustrated, angry, sad, distressed, crabby, resentful, unsatisfied, shall I go on?

All who follow God, always searching for Him, always telling Him you love Him, always wanting Him close to you, are ALWAYS happy.

Psalms 118:29 ESV... Oh, give thanks to the LORD, for He is SO good! For His loving kindness is FOREVER.

Blessed, favored, love and joyful...Memaw

A Servants Heart

Thursday's Thoughts: What Do You Serve?

According to the Bible, to serve is to be a devoted and helpful follower, to be humble before God, to be ready to act as God nudges and inspires us, to help meet the needs of other people, and to remember that it is not about money or reward. In a nutshell it means to minister.

But if you begrudge doing something for someone else it's not serving. What you define as a servant is how or who you serve. Your heart reveals what is servant and what is duty. Happy heart, servant heart. Angry heart, begrudging servant.

Love you all.

Blessing's favor and love...Memaw

Friday's Fruit: What Do You Invest In, And Who Do You Invest In?

Investing is expending something, money, time, or possessions, with the expectation of achieving a profit.

Proverbs 31:16...She considers a field and buys it; with the fruit of her hands, she plants a vineyard. The

Proverbs 31 woman invested in her family. Her profit was that her family was taken care of.

Luke 12:15 ESV. And he said to them, "Take care, and be on your guard against all covetousness, for one's life does not consist in the abundance of his possessions.

What you invest in, or who you invest in, is what your profit is.

Are you investing in yourself? If you are, your profit will be unsatisfaction. Invest in Jesus and you will never be unsatisfied again. Invest in your marriage, and you will gain a lifetime of happiness. (Not without trials but great rewards). Invest in your children and you will profit blessings beyond measure.

If you don’t believe me, try it and see what happens. Because God said it, I didn't.

Old saying from God's Word: Birds of a feather, flock together. Meaning: you believe the same thing, you do same things together, go to the same places.

Is the flock you keep of God?

Whatever you invest in is what you will profit. When you have to many things, you find you can't keep up with them. When you are going places and saying things contrary to God's Word you are rebelling and dishonoring God.

I am investing my life in you for Jesus...love you Memaw

I Surrender All

Saturday's Sayings: Surrendered Possessions

What do you possess or what possesses you? What is it that you have that you will not give up for anything?

It's called a sacrifice, which is: An act of surrendering a possession as an offering to God.

I guess this sermon is for me today.

You can tell if you won't give up certain things, or property, or even people, when you act like a starving dog over food, or a bone. It is a fight to the death. We snarl, growl, show our facial expression, grind our teeth, raise our hair on our necks, and put all four feet in position to attack. We will even attack God.

Sacrifice comes from the heart. Someone dropped a tiny crumb on my table once and felt terrible about it. They went on and on about how sorry they were. I looked at it intently and said, don't worry, I wasn't planning on carrying that to heaven with me.

What is it you possess that would cause you to lose a friend, break up a church, divide a family, ruin a relationship, close down good get togethers, or create animosity among people? Are our possessions worth that much to us?

This is my commandment, that you love one another as I have loved you. Greater love has no one than this, that someone lay down his life for his friends. You are my friends if you do what I command you" John 15:12-14 KJV

I love you.... Memaw

Crucified With Christ

Sunday's Song: What Faith Do You Live Your Life By?

I am crucified with Christ: nevertheless, I live; yet not I, but Christ liveth in me: and the life which I now live in the flesh, I live by the faith of the Son of God, who loved me, and gave himself for me. Galatians 2:20

Paul says in this verse that he lives by the faith "of" the Son of God. Do you live by the faith Jesus had?

1JOHN 4:7-9 KJV says; …for love is of God; and everyone that loveth is born of God, and knoweth God. He that loveth not, knoweth not God; for God is love. In this was manifested the love of God toward us, because God sent His only begotten Son into the world, that we might become alive through Him.

Again, God says here.... He sent Jesus for us to live through Him.

Do you believe what Jesus believes? Does your faith stand firm on what Jesus believed? Then I can't believe in what the world does, can I?

I believe what Jesus believes, I live because Jesus lives, and I love because He loves.

I Love you ...Memaw

Measured Walls

Monday's Meditations: What Do Your Walls Look like?

Are your walls strong and protective, visible so others can see that you are honorable and trustworthy, or are your walls hidden around the sin you are harboring?

In this day and age, walls can be viewed with negative connotations. Walls can be seen as a source of imprisonment and division. They are often referred to as things we need to break down and overcome.

However, when we look at walls in the bible, they are also seen as structures that protect, providing security, and represent a place of shelter and forming a sense of belonging.

When a parent tears down the walls around their family, their children become unprotected. To find that place of security and safety again our children begin to reach for people and things to fill that hurt empty spot in their life. Being immature and so confused they will let anyone that looks like love into their life. When a parent breaks down the family's wall for self, they have unleashed ALL of hells evil forces into their lives. Measure what's going on behind your walls and you will find who has gotten in.

Peace, joy, patience, kindness, self-control, measure your walls as secure.

Fighting, bickering, dishonesty, snapping at each other, vain thoughts measure broken walls.

Jerusalem's (your home) wall has been broken down, and its gates have been burned down.' When I heard these things, I sat down and wept. Nehemiah 1:3-4 NIV.

I will demolish the wall you plastered with whitewash and knock it to the ground so that its foundation is exposed. The city will fall, and you will be destroyed within it. Then you will know that I am the LORD. Ezekiel 13:14 TLB

You cannot tear down walls made of God. But it takes a lifetime to repair the walls you broke for self. And you NEVER get rid of the pain you cause your children. NEVER.

Father, in the Name of Jesus, help the children. Love Memaw

Living Respectable Lives

Tuesday's Tips: Where Are You?

1PETER 5:8-9 KJV...Your adversary, the devil walks around like a roaring lion, seeking whom he may devour.

Has Satan gotten a hold of you yet? He's looking for you. He is relentless in catching you. The next word Peter says is resist him. Satan is a liar, in fact God says he is the father of lies. You can tell who the daddy is by the way they live life.

I ask where are you? because 1JOHN 2:19 KJV says...they went out from us; for if they had been OF us, they would have no doubt have continued with us: but they went out (listen children) that it might be revealed that they were not of us.

Where are you? Are you in the body of Christ, or have you gone out from us? Is it being revealed that you were never truly part of Christ? Or, are you like so many others pretending to be a believer? So now Christ is in the way of the life you want.

There is a book I am reading called "Respectable Sins." It's about those sins that we have such respect for that we do them even though they dishonor God. Our Respectable sins quench the Holy Spirit in us because He is not really that important anyway. Show me the "friends" you keep, and I will show you your future.

Are your friends living the same Respectable life of sins you are? Jesus called this hypocrite.

The devil is against the living Christ and wants to destroy Him. If you are filled with the living Christ, the devil is eager to get you out of the way in order to destroy Christ's power in you. And your response should be: “now Lord, look after this property of Yours.” And the devil cannot get near you.

When does Satan get near you? When you dethrone Christ, ignoring His rightful position over you, in you and through you.

Always loving you...Memaw

True Bread

Wednesday's Word: Notes From Jesus

A picture of Jesus rising out of the tomb is a picture of us rising from the sin life to a life in Christ Jesus.

Temptation is a fight; it's not giving in.

You don't know how to win unless you go up against a fight or go through a fight.

You can't take earth to heaven, but you can bring heaven to earth.

If you don't know how much God loves you, you can't truly know how to love others.

John 1:1...the Word of God went forth and made things happen...as our words make things happen...good or bad.

Jesus chose Judas, but Judas never chose Jesus. Jesus had an influence that Judas wanted. He just belonged to the church and not Jesus.

John 6:58 NLT...I am the true bread from heaven and anyone who eats this bread shall live FOREVER and not die as your fathers died though they ate the bread from heaven.

They died in disobedience and unbelief. They turned their back on believing God would do what He said.

Taking note of my life...love Memaw

Thursday's Thoughts: Do You Know How Blessed You Are?

Blessed: divinely or supremely favored; fortunate to be blessed with a strong, healthy body; blessed with an ability to find friends. Blissfully happy or contented.

Divinely favored, do you know that you are favored by God?

Or is your life in your view so chaotic, that you can't even see how favored by God that you are? What about your eyes, when you woke up this morning, could you see things? Could you hear, could you talk, could you smell, walk, and sit without help? Do you have food? Are your children well? Are you in a safe place? People who don't have one or more of the things I just mentioned know how blessed they are. They know things could be worse. But they have the peace of God that they are blessed.

Philippians 4:8 KJV Finally, brethren, whatsoever things are true, whatsoever things are honest, whatsoever things are just, whatsoever things are pure, whatsoever things are lovely, whatsoever things are of good report; if there be any virtue, and if there be any praise, think on these things.

And you will know you are blessed.

With blessings of love...Memaw

A Mother's Prayer

Friday's Fruit: Praying For You

I pray, Lord, in the day of my children's troubles, may You Father be with them. I pray Father in Jesus name that You keep them from all harm. Father, send them Your aid from Your sanctuary in heaven. Father, may they remember with pleasure the gifts You have given them. I pray You grant them the desires of their hearts and fulfill all their plans. May I hear shouts of joy when I hear the news of their victory. And may I hear praise to You our God, for all that You have done for them. I pray that You Father answer all their prayers. I know You will. I know You hear me from Your highest heaven and send great victories. Some boasts in their possessions, but we boast in the Lord our God. People who don't know You will collapse and perish, but we will stand firm and sure. In the name of Jesus, give victory oh Lord, oh hear my prayer. Amen

Psalms 20 TL

God hears and answers His Word prayed. I love you Jesus....and children...Memaw

Life By Wisdom

Saturday's Sayings: Wisdom Or The Lack Of.

Proverbs 10 TLB

Ill-gotten gain brings no lasting happiness; right living does.

The Lord will not let a good man starve to death, nor will He let the wicked man's riches continue forever.

Lazy men are soon poor; hard workers get rich.

A wise person makes hay while the sun shines, but what a shame to see a person who sleeps away his hour of opportunity.

The wise man is glad to be instructed, but a self-sufficient fool falls flat on his face.

There is living truth in what a good man says, but the mouth of the evil man is filled with curses.

A wise person holds their tongue. Only a fool blurts out everything they know; that only leads to sorrow and trouble.

The good man's earnings advance the cause of righteousness. The evil man squanders his on sin.

Anyone willing to be corrected is on the pathway to life. Anyone refusing has lost his chance.

To hate is to be a liar. To slander is to be a fool.

From God and Memaw with love.

Learning The Hard Way

Sunday's Song: Can You Recognize Satan?

Let's first talk about Eve and Satan in the Garden of Eden. Satan disguised himself. He did not look like Satan or evil. He had a normal appearance to her human eyes, or she would have seen who he really was. He wasn't scary. He didn't display an evil demeanor. In fact, he presented himself as wise, thought-provoking, with great persuasion. Just normal looks, normal conversation, normal manners. But Eve didn't have a clue what Satan should look like.

Do you?

Do you know when you have encountered Satan?

Eve had not been taught anything about Satan or his evil ways. She learned of him the hard way.

How have you learned of Satan?

Nothing about Satan triggered who he was. Genesis 3:1-7 says Satan was the shrewdest (sharp thinker) of all the animals the Lord had made. He is cunning (deceptive) in asking Eve questions. He knew how to trip Eve up. And he hasn't changed a bit today. He still looks normal, still deceives, still trying to take you away from God.

1PETER 5:8 your adversary, Revelation 12:10 your accuser, Matthew 13:39 your enemy, John 8:44 father of lies, Matthew 12:43 your tempter.

Oh, and he has the power to enter any person that opens the door for him to do his work through, and it's not always wicked people. He does his best work through believers in Christ. If we neglect to learn his ways, we can be easily used by him.

He works mainly in families, then churches to divide them. He tricks you into believing that it's the person you are closest to, that's the problem. He loves to make you believe sin is ok. Believing other people’s sin is terrible, but yours is warranted.

When you realize what your sin did to Jesus, you will understand where sin comes from. Satan is your worst enemy, not the people in your life.

Just because my attitude thinks I am perfect doesn't make others imperfect.

Those people who hurt you was used by Satan, and if you want to hurt them back, you will be doing his work also.

Love Memaw

Followers Of Jesus

Monday's Meditations: What Kind Of Follower Are You?

Follow means to go or come after.

God taught me early this morning that follow, is a truth.

Whatever you believe you follow. Some follow their dreams. Some follow the path they are taught through how they were raised. Whether it's the Word of God, kindness, work ethics, alcohol, drugs or abuse. Some follow influence, looking at the life of a person of wealth or fame. Whatever people choose to follow that's what they believe as truth.

Jesus said follow Him. Follow His truth. Follow by going after how He lived. Follow by coming before God with a confidence in what His Word says. Follow with the same desires of Christ. His only desire was to do the will of His Father.

Do you realize that through Jesus you can come to God with the same assurance as Jesus? What an awesome example to Follow, to believe in, to come after, to go for.

Paul says: Follow my example, as I follow the example of Christ.

1CORITHIANS 11:1 NIV

You follow (come after or go after) what you believe in. So, what are you following, and who is following after you?

Whoever is following after you, what will they be going, or coming after?

Following the truth, Jesus...with love...Memaw

Humbled

Tuesday's Tips: What Humbles You?

Humble means having or showing a modest or low estimate of one's own importance. Memaws' definition is realizing you're not too big for your britches after all.

God says, If My people, (that's you) who are called by My Name, will humble themselves, and pray, and seek My face, and turn from their wicked ways, then I WILL hear from heaven, and I WILL forgive their sin and heal their land.

What's your problem? Are you truly called by God's Name? The only way you don't have God's Name is if you have not asked Jesus to be your Lord. Are you and your misery so important that you refuse to humble yourself by throwing yourself and those nasty hurts at the feet of Christ, who will intercede for you? Have you even prayed and asked God to help in Jesus' Name? Have you sought God to look at His creation with His mercy? Have you turned from your wicked ways? Anything you do by action and thought that is contrary to God's Word is sin. Even neglecting to do what is right is sin. God will not hear your prayers until you get rid of your sin. If God answered your prayers while you continued with your sinful life, He would be betraying Jesus, who took your sins on His life. You think God is going to betray His Son after He was beaten and hanged for you, while you hang on to your sin?

God says give up your sins and I WILL hear you. I WILL forgive you, and WHATEVER you need fixing, I WILL do it. I will heal your land. Your life, I will heal. Your health, I will heal. Your circumstances I will heal them all.

Pride stops humility. Unforgiving stops answers from God. Self-righteousness is opposite His righteousness. ALL sin stops God's work in your life. Humble yourself before God, not man, and He will keep His Word to you.

I humble myself before God for you...Love Memaw

The Fruit Of Your Labor

Wednesday's Word: How Are Things Going With You?

Need encouragement? Looking for a solution for all your labor? Been trying to figure out a better way to get help? Don't give up, just take a deep breath and read what God says about you.

Tell the righteous it will be well with them, for they will enjoy the fruit of their labor.
Isaiah 3:10

Peace on your journey there....love Memaw

Thursday's Thoughts: Tid Bits From The Lord And Memaw

A new commandment I give to you, that you love one another. John 13:34 NIV
(And not just the lovable)

Walk in love. Ephesians 5:2
(Not in anger)

Even in darkness, light dawns for the upright. Psalms 112:4
(Can't see the righteous way without His light)

God will bless you in everything you do, if you listen and obey. James 1:25
(Even during your trials, hurts and pain...through it ALL...YES JESUS THROUGH IT ALL)

The godly may trip seven times, but they will get up again. Proverbs 24:16
(Satan has no power to keep godly people from getting up again)

I told them many things....so they would be filled with My joy. John 17:13

(No Jesus, no joy)

Holy Spirit instruct my children in Christ today...love Memaw

Friday's Fruit: Are ALL Your Sins Covered By The Blood Of Christ Jesus?

Very early this morning, I woke up remembering a sin I had committed years ago. I immediately asked Christ to forgive me. Then I remembered I had already asked for forgiveness for this sin. So, to confirm that this sin and all my other sins are covered, I went to the author of the truth, God's Word, and sure enough, I found my answer.

Knowing that you were ransomed from the futile ways inherited from your forefathers, not with perishable things such as silver or gold, but with the precious blood of Christ, like that of a lamb without blemish or spot.
1PETER 1:18-19 ESV

Blessed are those whose lawless deeds are forgiven, and whose sins are covered.
Romans 4:7 ESV

Paul, through the Holy Spirit says in Romans 1, verses 18-20, TLB ... but God shows His anger from heaven against ALL sinful evil men who push away the truth from themselves. For the truth about God is known to them instinctively; God has put this knowledge in their hearts. Since earliest times men have seen the earth and sky and all God made and have known of His existence and great eternal power. So, they have no excuse when they stand before God on judgment day.

Paul goes on to say because they knew right from wrong but refuse to do it God let them go to do whatever they want to: every kind of wickedness and sin. But look at a few sins Paul mentions. Greed, hate, envy, murder, fighting, lying, bitterness, gossip, backbiters, haters of God, insolent (rude, lack of respect) proud, braggarts. There is coming a day of judgment on ALL who live like this. Are you covered? There will be NO excuse for ANYONE. Your lifestyle matters.

Covered by His blood...and love
..Memaw

Dressed For The King

Saturday's Sayings: What Does Your Dress Look Like?

Luke 12:32 NIV- it gives your Father great happiness to give you the Kingdom.

What is on this earth that you want that is greater than what is in God's Kingdom?

Verses 35-36 - be dressed for service and keep your lamps burning as though you were waiting for your Master to return from the wedding feast. Then you will be ready to open the door and let Him in the moment He arrives and knocks.

Are you dressed for service? Is your lamp burning with the Holy Spirit and are you following His guidance?

If Jesus came to your house, are you ready to open the door?

Get ready...He's coming.

Love Memaw

Good News

Sunday's Song: Are You A Slave, Truly A Slave Of Christ?

Paul, in the book of Romans says he was a slave of Christ. In chapters 1-2 which I have been reading all week. Paul says he is to preach the GOOD NEWS. This GOOD NEWS is God through His Son Christ Jesus who is the Holy NATURE of God poured out on us undeserving sinners His kindness. V17. This GOOD NEWS tells us God is making us ready for heaven. V18. But God shows His anger from heaven against ALL sinful people who push away the truth from themselves. Paul says the truth of God is known instinctively. God put this knowledge of Him in our hearts. So, they will have NO excuse when they, I stand before Him on judgment day. Paul says we know about Him, but we won't admit it or worship Him or even thank Him for all His daily care. In the rest of this chapter God lists some of the vile things people do. And Paul says because they were living wicked lives God lets them go and do these evil things. Watch out that you don't get the idea God is talking about someone else and not you. Because there are a couple of evil things God mentions that people do such as gossip, fight each other. And we still don't think this applies to us. In chapter 2, Paul says, wait a minute, YOU, ME are just as bad. In Psalms 119 God tells us to search our hearts and see if there is anything that doesn't line up with His Word. And repent of everything He points out that's in us. We want to think that the nation and world have gone to hell in a basket. But what are you doing differently that keeps you out of the basket to hell? DAILY examine yourself and let God change you.

In Jesus's Name...I love you, Memaw

Loved And Approved Of By God

Monday's Meditations: "Fearing People Is A Dangerous Trap"

If your life's goal is to have the approval of people, you will never feel secure. Why is that? Because the time will come when you do something that they disapprove of, then what? The Bible says, fearing people is a dangerous trap, but trusting the Lord means safety (Psalms 29:25) A trap is just another word for a prison. If someone other than God can determine your worth as a person, that someone can make you feel like a prisoner any time they decide to. When a critic's opinion becomes your own opinion, you're living in a prison of your own making. Face it: Some of the people you're trying so hard to impress will never be impressed. And you must accept this: From God's perspective, it doesn't matter. Knowing that enables you to work alongside people without allowing yourself to be controlled by their moods and governed by their opinions. Each time Paul went to another town, people were meeting and hearing him for the first time. Some of them liked him, and some didn't. He writes, "For some say, Paul's letters are demanding and forceful, but in person he is weak, and his speeches are worthless!" (2Cor. 10:10). So how did Paul handle this? He writes, "Obviously, I'm not trying to win the approval of people, but of God. If pleasing people were my goal, I would not be Christ's servant" (Gal. 1:10). In order to feel secure in life and fulfilled in what you're doing, you must reach the place where you can look in the mirror and say, "I'm loved and approved by God, and that's what matters!"

So good....love you Memaw

Think About Such Things

Tuesday's Tips: What Is Your Attitude Like?

A bad attitude is like a flat tire; it won't get better until you change it.

Your attitude needs constant adjustment. Anything you don't maintain eventually deteriorates.

Pray for God's help, because you will need it.

Look for the good, and you will find it.

Look for people who are of faith and spend time with them.

Where are these faith people? Soaring above the doubters like eagles.

Seven times a day David praised God. Psalms 119:164 Imagine what it would do for you.

Need something to think about to help your attitude?

If anything is excellent or praiseworthy - think about such things. Philippians 4:8 NIV

I think about you...love Memaw

The Attitude Of Christ

Wednesday's Word: Attitude (cont.)

Your attitude is like the engine that runs the car. The more finely tuned that engine is, the better the car will run. ~ Keith Harrell

Excellence is not a skill. It is an attitude. ~ Ralph Marston

Attitudes are the forerunners of conditions. ~ Eric Butterworth

The greatest discovery of my generation is that a human being can alter his life by altering his attitudes. ~ William James

Great effort springs naturally from a great attitude. ~ Pat Riley

And last, your attitude is sometimes like a stinky diaper that needs changing.

1Peter 4:1 NIV Therefore, since Christ suffered in His body, arm yourselves also with the same attitude, because whoever suffers in the body is done with sin.

Romans 15:5 NIV May the God who gives endurance and encouragement give you the same attitude of mind toward each other that Christ Jesus had,

Blessings with the attitude of Christ Jesus...love Memaw

A Blameless Life

Thursday's Thoughts: Who May Go To The LORD?

Lord, who may go and find refuge and shelter in Your Tabernacle up on Your Holy hill?

Anyone who leads a blameless life and who is truly sincere. Anyone who refuses to slander others, does not listen to gossip, never harms his neighbor, speaks out against sin, criticizes those committing it, commends the faithful followers of the Lord, keeps a promise even if it ruins him, does not crush his debtors with high interest rates, and refuses to testify against the innocent despite the bribes offered him - and such a man shall stand firm forever. Psalms 15. TLB

How does your life stand before the Lord?

Love you...Memaw

The Test Of Faith

Friday's Fruit: Heavy Heart

Search me, God, and know my heart; test me and know my anxious thoughts. See if there is any offensive way in me and lead me in the way everlasting. Psalms 139:23-24

Test yourself to see if you are in the faith; examine yourselves! Or do you not recognize this about yourselves, that Jesus Christ is in you—unless indeed you failed the test. 2CORITHIANS 13:5 NASV

Do you have offensive thoughts? If you don't, then there should never be unkind thoughts about each other. Jesus will never think mean thoughts about us. No matter what we have done, He never thinks bad about us. He died to make us a family. What happened? The love of Christ in each of us should be more than enough to love each other. So, examine yourselves and see if He is really in you. We get so tangled in what one of us did or didn't do that we put such a thick cover over the love of Jesus in us that we can't love them. What's it going to take for each of us to love each other? What needs to happen before Jesus' love flows through and out of you? I have searched myself, and I have found resentment, self-centeredness, and bitterness just to name these 3, and I am ashamed that I wanted you to see Jesus in me on the outside but couldn't find Him on the inside. Where can I find Him?

I love you, your Mom, and Memaw

Growing In Jesus

Saturday's Sayings: Are You Growing In Christ?

Are you growing in His Word?

Are you growing in His promises?

Matthew 5:3 NIV- Blessed are the poor in spirit, for theirs is the kingdom of God.

Strange verse to use to ask if you are growing in Christ, but being poor in spirit is seeing the sin in your life and not the sin of others. Seeing your sin grows you to seek God's forgiveness. Being poor without being forgiven is staying in your old life. Growing means moving into another place with Christ.

Again, are you growing?

Growing in Jesus...Love Memaw

Redeemed Through Mercy

Sunday's Song: God Says

All those who know Your mercy, Lord, will count on You for help. For You have never yet forsaken those who trust in You. Psalms 9:10

Do you truly KNOW God's mercy?

Oh God, You have declared me perfect in Your eyes, You have ALWAYS cared for me in my distress, now hear me as I call again. Have mercy on me. Hear my prayer. Psalms 4:1

Mark this well; The Lord has set apart the redeemed for Himself. Therefore, He will listen to me and answer when I call to Him. Psalms 4:3 TLB

Are you redeemed? Are you set apart for Him, or does someone else use you? Do you truly know God?

Redeemed with love...Memaw

THANK YOU.

About The Author

My name is Reba Mason, and I'm the wife of Jimmy Mason, the mother of two grown daughters, grandmother to thirteen grandchildren, and great grandmother to twenty-four, and counting.

I was born in Pike County, Alabama, but raised in the small rural town of Brantley, AL. I am the oldest child of Edward and Mavis Mount.

My hobbies are gardening, hosting bible home groups and learning everything about God's Word on how to live out my life before Him and others.

As a small child, life was very hard. My daddy died when I was twenty months old, which left my mom with three babies to raise. Since I was the oldest, I became her helper. Such as getting toys, diapers or bottles for either my brother or sister while she took care of the one needing attention. Along with keeping house, cooking meals, milking cows and washing clothes. We had no car, telephone, electricity, running water and no bathroom inside. All the necessities of life during those early years were obtained from using your hands and Gods earth. We grew everything we ate except flour and sugar. Those items we bought from what was called a "rolling store." This rolling store was a large, covered vehicle that went around the countryside selling various items that people might need because they had no transportation other than a mule and wagon. As I said earlier, there was no car or truck on the farm. The rolling store was similar to what we call a van today. You traded eggs or chickens for flour and sugar because those items were not grown on our farm.

By the time I turned six we had moved into town for me to start school. And as you read some of the pages of this book, it will explain some of what my life as a child was like.

Now at age 79, and a new creation in Christ, the old has passed away. In Christ, nothing from the difficult, scary, embarrassing, shameful, abusive, or traumatic events from my younger life matters. I am who God says I am. I have learned that none of my past life was forever, even though for many years it seemed as if it was, but I have learned that only Christ and in Him is forever.

So, I hope as you finished reading this book that you realized from my journey in life, that I was a broken pearl that became part of Jesus' Crown.

And this is the confidence that we have in Him, that if we ask anything according to His will, He hears us, and if we know that He hears us, we know that we have the petition that we desired of Him. 1John 5:14-15 KJV

www.ingramcontent.com/pod-product-compliance
Lightning Source LLC
LaVergne TN
LVHW020702110826
845149LV00012B/2071

9781968766153